T0302265

There are a lot of books on the market about high performance and lot of them contain waffle. I like to keep things simple. This book is succinct and perfectly describes the different aspects of performance required to maintain it at its peak. What's more, it is backed up by real examples – evidence.

Shaun Wane, Head Coach, England Rugby League

Peak Performance Every Time

Most people have good days ... and not so good days. When they step back and ask what makes the difference, many conclude that it's that stuff that happens between their ears. So, how do we engineer our mindset? How do we get our mental game right, so that we can perform at our best, consistently?

Peak Performance Every Time provides readers with a detailed look into how to build the critical components of a great mental game. It will help them to hone their focus, control their confidence, master motivation and deliver their best 'under pressure'. In short, it will help deliver peak performance, every time. The book provides a practical guide to performance psychology, based on approaches and methods that have been tried and tested in the demanding world of elite sport. In addition to applied practice, it provides real life examples and case studies from both elite sport and business, plus the underpinning theory and research.

This book will be invaluable to anyone trying to reach their full potential, in particular athletes, coaches, managers and executives. It may also be of interest to sports psychology, management and business students.

Simon Hartley is a world-renowned sport psychology consultant and performance coach. For over 25 years, Simon has worked with Olympians, world champions, world record holders and championship winning teams. He has worked at the highest level of sport, including spells in Premier League and Bundesliga football, Premiership rugby union, Formula One and International Cricket. Since 2005, Simon has also applied the principles of sport psychology to business with some of the world's leading corporations and delivers keynotes across the globe.

Peak Performance Every Time

Strategies for Confidence, Motivation, and Focus

Second Edition

SIMON HARTLEY

Routledge
Taylor & Francis Group

LONDON AND NEW YORK

Cover image: © Getty Images

Second edition published 2024
by Routledge
4 Park Square, Milton Park, Abingdon, Oxon, OX14 4RN

and by Routledge
605 Third Avenue, New York, NY 10158

Routledge is an imprint of the Taylor & Francis Group, an informa business

© 2024 Simon Hartley

First edition published by Routledge 2011

British Library Cataloguing-in-Publication Data
A catalogue record for this book is available from the British Library

ISBN: 978-1-032-02021-1 (hbk)
ISBN: 978-1-032-02019-8 (pbk)
ISBN: 978-1-003-18149-1 (ebk)

DOI: 10.4324/9781003181491

Typeset in Dante and Avenir
by SPi Technologies India Pvt Ltd (Straive)

Contents

Acknowledgments

Thank you to my wonderful wife, my beautiful girls, my incredibly support-ive family, and my fantastic friends.

I would also like to thank England Rugby League Head Coach, Shaun Wane, for writing the Foreword, and the team at Taylor and Francis for their help and support.

Biography

Simon Hartley is a world-renowned sport psychology consultant and performance coach. He helps individuals, teams and organizations to get their mental game right. For over 25 years, Simon has worked with gold medalists, world record holders and championship winning teams. He has worked at the highest level of sport, including spells in Premier League and Bundesliga football, Premiership rugby union, Formula One, International Cricket, Super League, golf, tennis, and with dozens of Great British Olympians.

Since 2005, Simon has also applied the principles of sport psychology to business, education and beyond. He now works with some of the world's largest corporations and delivers keynotes throughout the globe.

Foreword

Shaun Wane

I am lucky that I have not needed to work a day in my life. I enjoy my 'work' so much that I do not consider it to be 'work'. I never thought it was possible to achieve what I have, due to where I started in life. Being able to play and coach my home-town team to success was a dream come true.

Having a clear and concise purpose and goal makes what you do, easy. In sport, it is a little easier to work out what that goal is – in my case, winning a Grand Final, year on year. In business it might take some more working out. However, once you know what that is, your passion and commitment to the cause will shine through. This mixture is the driving force which will create something extraordinary.

I don't just experience this in my career as a Head Coach in Rugby League, I get this sense of purpose in most things I do. I think that is because I enjoy the process and challenge of achieving something. I feel comfortable in spaces which other people find *un*-comfortable. I don't mind having what others perceive as difficult conversations.

I met Simon many years ago and have been in regular contact ever since. This is because we have so many similar beliefs. Simon's book *Peak Performance Every Time*, is incredibly closely aligned with my beliefs as a coach, and as a person. This book eloquently describes some incredibly important contributors to success, many of which I have experienced during my most successful times as a Head Coach.

There are a lot of books on the market about high performance and a lot of them contain waffle. I like to keep things simple. This book is succinct and perfectly describes the different aspects of performance required to maintain it at its peak. What's more, it is backed up by real examples – evidence.

When you experience the combination of aspects of performance described in this book, I truly believe that it is in this space that magic happens. Read it and achieve it.

Preface

When I started my journey in sport psychology, over 25 years ago, I did what most people do. I began by trying to apply the knowledge that I had learned in the classroom. I took the textbook theories and the research into the field.

In the world of elite sport, there is a simple, hard truth. What you do *has* to work! It has to make a positive impact. It has to achieve the desired result. Therefore, the tools that I put in my toolbox were the ones I could rely on to get the best possible results, quickly, effectively and consistently. At the highest level of sport, there is little margin for error. My experiences in Premier League and Bundesliga football, Premiership rugby union, Super League, NFL, International and First Class cricket, Olympic sports, golf, tennis and motor sport all emphasize the critical importance of using strategies that work. The reality is that there is often a hair's breadth between winning and losing, but that the difference in the rewards can be astronomical.

Obviously, this is not just true of elite sport. It is also true in business and many other realms. Over the last quarter of a century, I've applied exactly the same approaches with entrepreneurs, global corporations, in education, healthcare, the military and many other walks of life.

Initially it took me a while to understand why it had worked so well. I was puzzled as to how sport psychology applied so easily to other environments. The answer of course is very simple. There is a simple common denominator. We are all humans.

Some of the approaches I now use with athletes and sports teams come from business environments, the military, aviation, surgery, education and mainstream psychology. Experience has taught me the value of working from real life back to the textbook. Put simply, I find what works, and then align it with the science.

I have included the references so that you can explore some of these incredibly valuable resources for yourself. The final chapter of the book identifies some of the theory and research that underpins these methods.

This book explains how to apply performance coaching strategies to your life. To help the ideas come to life, I've used some live examples from my work with athletes, sports teams, executives and business organizations. I genuinely hope that you find these as useful as I have, and that they have a positive impact on your performance and your life.

Introduction

Everyone wants to win.

But not everyone will win.

Many people say that the difference between the best and the rest is 'mindset'.

But what do we mean by the word mindset?

In my experience, when most people talk about mindset, they're referring to the moment-by-moment flow of thoughts and feelings.

Do they feel confidence or doubt?

Does the voice in their head say, 'Give it a go' or 'Forget it. You've got no chance?'

To be honest, that's the way I once saw it too. When I wrote the first edition of this book, a decade ago, that's what I focused on. Today, I refer to our moment-by-moment thinking and emotion as 'our mental game'. I used to think that this was the extent of our mindset. However, during the last decade, I've come to appreciate that there is another dimension, which drives our mental game.

I've also come to realize that managing our mindset is simple, but not necessarily easy. Like with many things, it falls into the 'easier said than done category'.

The truth is, your performance is entirely within your control. Your performance is not dictated by anyone else or anything else. It's not dictated by circumstances or external factors. Your performance emanates from your thoughts and feelings. Nobody can influence your thoughts or feelings, unless you let them! No situation or circumstance can impact on your thoughts or feelings, unless you allow it (Manz, 2000).

You have ultimate control over how you think and feel. Therefore, you have ultimate control over your performance.

DOI: 10.4324/9781003181491-1

As Viktor Frankl (1959/1984) says, the ability to choose what we think and how we feel is "the last of our human freedoms". He learned that it's possible to do that in one of the most extreme and horrific environments humanity has ever seen – in Auschwitz.

So why is it that so many people, including elite athletes, struggle to control their mind and emotions? Why is it that so many of us are affected by circumstances and other people?

The fact is we all have the power to control our mind and emotions. However, most people give their power away.

Many years ago, I worked with a squad of elite junior fencers. The Director of Fencing initially approached me because the athletes were displaying a great deal of frustration and anger on the piste (the piste is the fencing equivalent of a pitch or a court. It is the narrow strip that they compete on). The problem is that if they display their frustration during competition, they risk being 'black carded' (disqualified) and banned from the competition for several months.

I started by talking with the fencers about the things which made them frustrated. They listed a host of factors that affected them. One athlete said that when the opponent celebrates, it really wound him up. Another said that if he was fighting an opponent who he was 'supposed to beat easily', he would get frustrated when they scored a point against him. Others were affected by the referee, the opponent's supporters, or their trash talk. At the end of the discussion, I asked them who had control over their mindset and their emotions. It was obvious that the fencers had given control of their own thoughts and feelings to just about everyone else. As a result, they were being ruled by other people and by circumstance. They had strapped themselves into a mental and emotional roller coaster because they had given up control.

The fencers needed to take back control.

We have control until we give it over to someone else or something else.

Through the course of this book, I will show you how to engineer the four key elements of your mental game. We will discover how to:

- Control confidence
- Master motivation
- Hone focus
- Deconstruct pressure

I will help you to take control over your mind and your emotions, and therefore, help you to engineer your performance. Your performance should not be left to chance. Many people's performance is subject to a host of variables. Too many people say, "I hope I'll do okay today". I'd argue that *hoping* is not enough. Wouldn't you rather *know* that you're going to perform well? Wouldn't you rather *know* that you have the ability to control your mind and your emotions? If you have control of your thoughts and feelings, you have a very good chance of producing a peak performance.

Most athletes, and indeed most people, would say that their aim is to win. The same is often true in business. We have targets and goals to achieve, and we are focused on hitting them.

But it doesn't always happen.

In both sport and business, often there can only be one winner. So, most people tend to set themselves a different stall. They are satisfied if they have performed at their peak, and disappointed if they drop short. World class performers in any discipline are normally dissatisfied with a below par performance even if they do win. Although no one likes losing, they will often be content if they lost but produced their very best performance on the day. If this is true for most of us, then our true aim is probably to achieve our potential and produce our peak performance.

> When I go out and race, I'm not trying to beat opponents, I'm trying to beat what I have done .. to beat myself, basically. People find that hard to believe because we've had such a bias to always strive to win things. If you win something and you haven't put everything into it, you haven't actually achieved anything at all. When you've had to work hard for something and you've got the best you can out of yourself on that given day, that's where you get satisfaction from.
>
> Ian Thorpe, Australian Olympic Swimmer

As a sport psychology consultant and performance coach, this is my aim. People often ask me how I help to boost people's performances. I guess many people imagine that I magically inject them with some kind of mental rocket fuel. Some people imagine that I hypnotize people to give them superhuman abilities. Obviously neither of these is true. I often explain to people that my job does not involve magic wands. I do not have any mental rocket packs. My job is not to give a performer anything they don't already have. In a sense, my role is not to enhance anything. Instead, my job is to take away the things that stop them from producing their potential.

> "Performance = Potential – Interference".
>
> (Gallwey, 1986)

As a performance coach, my job is to minimize the interference. Instead of strapping a mental rocket pack to you, my aim is simply to release the hand brake.

This interference, or baggage as it's sometimes called, comes from all sorts of sources. One of the most common sources is fear. Fear of failure. Fear of success. Fear of letting someone else down. Fear of looking daft. Fear of what other people will think of you if you screw up. Many people's performance is affected by a host of outside issues and agendas that they bring into play. In reality, our mental agendas have nothing whatsoever to do with the performance, but we allow them in and invite them to affect our mind and emotions.

Throughout the following chapters, we will also look at where this interference comes from and how to minimize it. We will learn how to stop creating it, and how to dismantle it.

This is where we step into the deeper dimensions of our mindset and understand what drives our mental game. To do this, we need to understand two critical components.

- Character
- Identity

During a conversation with a martial artist, he told me about feeling pressure to live up to everyone else's expectations. As we discussed it further, the athlete told me how he'd been bullied for a long time as a child and young adult. As a result, he had a real desire to prove himself to everyone else and show them how successful he was. This all acts as baggage. In reality, this agenda has nothing to do with his fight. It has nothing to do with the moves he has to make, how he counters the opponents' moves, or how he executes his technique. Instead, it acts as baggage, pulling his focus away from the important things that will allow him to perform. Instead of focusing on what he needs to do, he worries about what will happen if he fails.

The solution is pretty simple. He just needs to change his point of focus. Instead of worrying about what everyone else thinks, he simply needs to focus on the fight. But that's easier said than done.

The weight of expectation and fear of failure were probably bigger adversaries than his opponent. It's the same for many people.

So, how does he disentangle himself from the expectations, defuse the fear and unlock his true potential?

One answer is to develop courage. Courage is a characteristic – an element of our character. It is often described as our ability to step towards those things that scare us. So, to help this athlete focus on his performance, he may have to develop courage.

Another answer is to build a solid foundation of self-belief and self-worth, so that he doesn't need external validation. Self-belief and self-worth are elements of our identity.

The experience of this martial artist highlights how our mental game (the ability to hone our focus, control confidence and master motivation), is driven by deeper aspects of our mindset, such as character and identity.

So, where do we start? How do you start taking control over your mind and emotions? What's the first step?

Fundamentally, you need to have two things.

First, you need *awareness*. You need to know yourself and understand yourself. You need to know how your mind and emotions tend to work. We're all different and there is no blueprint to work from. However, we can all learn about our mental and emotional patterns simply by reflecting on what we do, what we say, how we think and how we feel (Wan, 2009; Hatzomoysis, 2010).

The second element is *responsibility*. We need to take responsibility for our thoughts and feelings. Once we take responsibility, we stop blaming other people or circumstances for how we feel (Jauncey, 2002). We need to recognize that if someone says something that makes us feel angry, scared, upset or uncomfortable, we have allowed that person to control our emotions.

We handed them the remote!

We ultimately have the ability to control how we feel. Therefore, it is not the other person's fault we feel bad, it is our responsibility to take control. There is a strong relationship between responsibility and control (Koestenbaum & Block, 2001; Martin Fischer & Ravizza, 1998; Nesti, 2004).

When we take responsibility, we can take control.

Changing your mindset and taking control of your thoughts and emotions, are not things that you can do at the click of your fingers. These are things that need to be learned. Normally, learning takes time. Inevitably, it requires us to make mistakes. As human beings we learn everything in the same way we learned to walk. We use the same basic tools and go through the same processes (Gallwey, 1986; Cook, 2005).

If you've ever watched babies learn to walk you will notice that they all fall over. In fact, they fall over a lot. Falling over is essential. Without falling over, they would not learn to walk. Babies are incredibly smart learners. For a start, you'll notice that they very rarely fall over the same way twice. That is because they constantly refine what they do and try it slightly differently each time.

I'd recommend banning the following phrase …

"If at first you don't succeed, try, try again".

I would suggest replacing it with this …

"If at first you don't succeed, change and try again … then change it and try again".

If we follow that simple formula, we will eventually succeed. As adults we often don't follow that formula. Instead, we get upset if we try three or four times and fail. If we fail enough times we give up. Babies have no concept of failure. To them, falling over is not failure. Because of this, babies don't reach a point where they consider giving up. They keep trying, changing and trying again until they get it right. We still have that incredible ability to learn. The only thing standing in our way is our perception of failure.

Imagine if Humphry Davy, Joseph Wilson Swan and Thomas Edison had given up when inventing the light bulb? What if they had tried a dozen times without success, and decided to give up? What if they had become despondent after 100 failed trials, or 1000? Edison trialed thousands of different materials for his filament before he had a commercially viable light bulb.

"A journey of 1000 miles starts with a single step".

In fact, a journey of 1000 miles is entirely composed of single steps. If you can take one step, simply repeat that step many times and you can walk 1000 miles. Taking control of your mind and emotions is a step-by-step process. It is a journey that can only be walked one step at a time. Your path towards engineering your peak performance consistently is a series of very manageable single steps. Like the journey of 1000 miles, it takes time and perseverance. Everyone is capable of making the journey as long as they keep taking the steps and learning the way they learned as a baby.

In summary …

- You have ultimate control over your thoughts and emotions.
- Only you can give that control away.
- When we take responsibility, we take control.
- Understanding ourselves is vital.
- It all takes time and requires mistakes. When learning to walk we must expect to fall over.

References

Cook, M. (2005) *The FreeFlow Method*, Northumberland, UK: SportsCoach21.

Frankl, V.E. (1959/1984). *Man's Search For Meaning*, New York: Touchstone.

Gallwey, T. (1986) *The Inner Game of Tennis*, London: Pan Books.

Hatzomoysis, A. (2010) *Self-Knowledge*, New York: Oxford University Press USA.

Jauncey, P. (2002) *Managing Yourself & Others*, Brisbane: CopyRight Publishing.

Koestenbaum, P. and Block, P. (2001) *Freedom and Accountability at Work: Applying Philosophic Insight to the Real World*, New York: Jossey Bass.

Manz, C.C. (2000) *Emotional Discipline: The Power to Choose How You Feel,* San Francisco: Berrett-Koehler.

Martin Fischer, J. and Ravizza, M. (1998) *Responsibility and Control: A Theory of Moral Responsibility,* Cambridge: Cambridge University Press.

Nesti, M.S. (2004) *Existential Psychology and Sport: Theory and Application,* Oxford: Routledge.

Wan, S. (2009) *Knowledge of Self: Impossible is Nothing,* Charleston, SC: CreateSpace.

In The Zone   1

"The zone".

That magical space where everything seems easy ... those moments when you're in 'flow' ... when you seem to have the Midas touch.

It is a state of complete concentration and total absorption. People often report that peak performances seem effortless. They seem to have more time, see things more clearly and find the performance easy. Everything they seem to attempt comes off (Jackson & Csikszentmihalyi, 1999).

But how do we get into this 'magical' state?

Research into 'the zone' tells us that there are a number of consistent features. 'The zone' is a state in which we are completely involved in an activity for its own sake. We lose our self in the task. We become immersed. Simply doing the activity becomes its own reward. Psychologists term this as *optimal intrinsic motivation*. It refers to a state where our whole being is involved in the task. We are so focused on the activity that we have almost no way of being distracted. There is no spare attention for anything else. In fact, there is probably not enough attention to even focus on our self (Jackson & Csikszentmihalyi, 1999).

It is noticeable that many accounts of peak performances talk about people becoming 'at one with the task'. In essence, their sense of self seems to recede. Their ego steps back into the shadows and they lose themselves in the activity. This often leads people to lose track of time. They report that hours seem like minutes. This is illustrated by an account of a composer.

DOI: 10.4324/9781003181491-2

That timelessness aspect of flow is so true! When I compose, I sometimes sit at the piano for over four hours without realizing a moment
has gone by! It used to be that way with practicing other composers'
work, but that lost a bit of its 'flow' magic after 15 years or so! It truly is
one of the weirdest and most rewarding feelings in the world out there!

(Pureakero, 2008)

Many people also describe a performance where every action, movement and
thought flows inevitably from the previous one. It is a heightened state of
consciousness where attention is extremely focused. It has been described as
the state of mind where attention and motivation meet.

A special place where performance is exceptionally consistent, automatic and flowing. An athlete is able to let his or her body deliver the
performance it has learned so well.

(Murphy, 1996: 4)

As you can imagine, accounts like these might be expected from elite athletes. However, peak performances are a feature of any walk of life. There
are many reports from surgeons, artists and musicians. Mihaly Csikszentmihalyi, the principal researcher of flow states and peak experiences, has con-
ducted over 8,000 interviews with those who have experienced being *in flow*.
His interviews cross occupations, demographic groups and cultures. They
include accounts from Dominican monks, blind nuns, Himalayan climbers
and Navajo shepherds.

Here are a few accounts given by people describing their experience of being
in flow. They are taken from a Keynote that Mihaly Csikszentmihalyi delivered
to a TED (Technology Education Design) Conference on 24 October 2008.

Music Composer

You are in an ecstatic state to such a point that you feel as though you
almost don't exist. I have experienced this time and again. My hand
seems devoid of myself, and I have nothing to do with what's happen-
ing. I just sit there watching it in a state of awe and wonderment. And
the music just flows out of itself.

Poet

It's like opening a door that's floating in the middle of nowhere and all
you have to do is go and turn the handle, and open it and let yourself

sink into it. You can't particularly force yourself into it. You just have to float. If there is any gravitational pull, it is from the outside world trying to keep you back from the door.

Figure Skater

It was just one of those programs that clicked. I mean, everything just went right, everything felt good … it's just such a rush, like you feel it could go on and on and on, like you don't want it to stop because it's going so well. It's like you don't have to think, it's like everything goes automatically without thinking … it's like you're on autopilot so you don't have any thoughts. You hear the music but you're not aware that you're hearing it, because it's a part of it all.

Bob Beamon reported such a heightened state of concentration during his world record long jump of 29 feet 2½ inches at the 1968 Summer Olympics in Mexico City. It was more than two feet farther than the previous world record. Incredibly, his record then stood for over 20 years until Mike Powell broke it in 1991. Looking back and trying to explain his 1968 jump, Beamon described it this way:

There is no answer for the performance. But everything was just perfect for it, the runway, my takeoff – I went six feet in the air when usually I'd go about five – and my concentration was perfect. It never happened quite that way before. I blocked out everything in the world, except my focus on the jump.

(Berkow, 1984)

Although we've looked at examples from specific disciplines, peak performances are not limited to any particular fields. You have the potential to experience peak performances in almost anything you do. During your life, you will have experienced moments where you've been 'in the zone'. You may have been writing something, cooking, negotiating a deal, doing a presentation or building something. The task is irrelevant. Even some apparently mundane tasks can provide people with peak experiences. Mihaly Csikszentmihalyi (2008) gives an example of a man whose job it is to slice fish. Slicing fish may not seem like a particularly engaging task. However, he dedicates his professional life to slicing his fish perfectly. He constantly pushes himself to perfect his technique and ensure that he slices evenly and consistently, following the striations on the flesh. The chef sees his job as an art form, like a sculptor.

I have used this same principle when working with a café restaurant chain. Most people waiting tables or serving food in a busy café wouldn't necessarily focus on achieving a peak performance. Many of the roles would probably be viewed as unskilled or menial. Most waiting staff probably start their shift with the primary aim of getting through it and going home as quickly as possible. However, we sought to adopt a different approach.

As the song says ... "It's not what you do, it's the way that you do it".

I discovered that there are a lot of skilled roles in a café. Making a coffee is a prime example. There are around a dozen steps to making a perfect espresso shot, all of which have to be executed exceptionally well in order to produce a great coffee. In addition, for a latte or cappuccino, there is a great deal of skill required to get the milk to the optimal consistency and texture. No wonder there is a World Championship for Baristas (Hartley, 2012).

Our job was not to make coffee. Our job was to make truly great coffee, and to take pride in the quality of coffee that we produced. We had internal competitions for our baristas and sent them on training courses to teach them how to make ever better coffee. The same was true of baking bread, preparing smoothies and juices, serving customers, cooking and presenting food, and even wiping down tables. How many tables have you seen in restaurants that aren't quite clean? How many servers have you seen wiping crumbs onto the floor or onto a chair? It seems like a very simple task and yet few people manage to execute it consistently well in the middle of a manic Saturday lunchtime shift. As with most things, it is easy to do the job poorly. It's both more challenging, and more rewarding, when we do the job really well.

By this point, you will no doubt have noticed a number of recurring themes. Peak performances tend to occur when there are several key ingredients present. The first is clear focus. It is very hard to have complete concentration on something if you don't have a clear focus. In *flow states*, action and awareness merge when there is total immersion in the task. This immersion is only possible when you have a genuine love for what you do and are happy to throw yourself into it, lock, stock and barrel. Focus follows interest (Gallwey, 2003). In order to be 100 percent focused on an activity, you have to want to do it purely for its own sake.

In order for many of the other ingredients to fall into place, you will need to be confident, excited, energized and in a pretty good mood. However, there are two other elements that are necessary for a person to truly achieve a peak performance. There needs to be a balance between the challenge presented and the skills of the individual. More specifically, there needs to be a balance between the challenge that the individual perceives, and the level of skill that they believe they have. When we have a level of challenge that really pushes us, and the skills to be able to display mastery, we stand a very good chance of performing to our potential. We need to be stretched to the limits of our capacity, but we also need to be confident that we have the ability to master the task. If we have the challenge but not the belief in our skills, we will experience anxiety. If we have the skills but we don't perceive that it is a stimulating challenge, we will become bored (Jackson & Csikszentmihalyi, 1999).

In the café restaurant business, we sought to increase the level of challenge by continually raising the standards and asking for greater and greater attention to detail. Where we asked people to engage in tasks that they were unfamiliar with, we made sure that they learned the skills fully. This ensured that they were confident in their ability and knew that they could deliver the standards that we expected. Many athletes I work with describe this as having 'trust' in their skills (Gallwey, 1986). When they trust, they are able to operate in that mindless state where they think less, stop trying and *just do it*.

The examples from the café business are typical of everyday life. We're not all composers, poets or elite athletes. Nonetheless, we have the opportunity to excel in what we do. You will have probably experienced peak performances in your life. You will have surprised yourself with something that you did. It might have been while playing sport. It may have been while working or engaged in a hobby. You may have regular and prolonged experiences of peak performances, or they may have only been fleeting glimpses.

Think back to peak moments. Have you been doing a task and become completely absorbed in it to the point where you lose track of time? Did you start to feel as if everything started to flow and almost become automatic? Did you do things so well that you surprised yourself? Did you do things you didn't realize you could do or that you'd not planned to do? If you've experienced some of these, you would probably describe it as a peak performance.

For most people, peak experiences are the exception, not the norm. More often than not, our performances are tinged with frustration. Things don't quite come off as we'd hoped. The performance is not exactly effortless and flowing. Instead, we experience interference. We question, we doubt, we overthink and overanalyze. We become overly aware of our thoughts and our frustrations (Nideffer, 2007). It's a far cry from losing our self in our activity. In contrast we are only connected to the activity very loosely, by a very thin thread. In fact, our connection often breaks, we force ourselves to reconnect, then it breaks again and so on. The whole process becomes laborious and fragmented (Flegal & Anderson, 2008).

So, how do we get into 'the zone'?

And, once we're there, how do we avoid falling out of it?

Experience tells me that *trying* to get into 'the zone' is completely counter-productive. Thinking more and trying harder often have the polar opposite effect. I've come to realize that we 'slip into the zone', or "sink into it", as the poet described.

Through the course of the following eleven chapters, we will look at how we can control our internal environment to allow ourselves to experience peak performances consistently and regularly. The environment we create will either allow us to flourish or struggle. Imagine a garden that is enclosed indoors. If you create an ideal climate, life will flourish. If the environment is too hot, too cold, too dry or too wet, life will struggle. We will look at the fundamental conditions that allow peak performances to flourish and how you can control them. In the following chapters, we will look primarily at how to control focus, confidence and motivation. We will also look at how to control the interferences that normally prevent people from experiencing a peak performance, such as fear and pressure.

There's lots of advice that sounds simple, but many people find fiendishly difficult to do.

"Don't think, just play"
"Just focus on the task"
"Don't worry"
"Don't focus on the negatives"

Experience tells me that there are very few techniques, tricks or skills, that genuinely help us control our thoughts and emotions (Corlett, 1996). Many people would advocate using techniques such as visualization or imagery. However, being able to imagine success tends to have very little impact on a person who is bricking themselves about a performance (Nesti, 2004). Positive thinking probably won't make a significant impact either. There is normally a reason why the person is scared. Sometimes, we have to dig a little deeper to actually address these issues and truly change our thoughts and feelings (Nesti, 2004).

Fundamentally, we have to know who we are (Frankl, 1959/1984). We have to know ourselves and be happy with ourselves (Seligman, 2005). We have to be comfortable in our own skin and with our lives if we are going to truly lose our self in an activity (Csikszentmihalyi, 1990). We need to be happy to step away from the ego that most of us rely upon to present a front to the world. Our ego is the part of us which projects our outward image. It's the part of our psyche that's concerned about how we look and what others think of us. We use the ego to give the world an impression of who we want to be. For many people, that impression may not be consistent with who we believe we are (Metzinger, 2010). Our ego wants to show the world how successful we are, even though we might be penniless. Our ego wants the world to think we look good, even though we might believe we're ugly, or fat, or misshapen. So, it's not always easy for us to abandon ego, lose our self-consciousness and leap headlong into an activity

> ... especially if someone is watching us
> ... especially if the outcome is important to us and the task is something we identify our self with
> ... and especially if we care about what other people think.

A few years ago, I was asked to work with a Super League, rugby league player. This particular player was the star of his team. He was their highest paid player and their big name. Unfortunately, he was experiencing a poor run of form. He was making mistake after mistake and his confidence was eroding fast. Here is a short piece from one of the session summaries I sent him.

> As we finished up the session, we started talking about the bigger issues that tend to be the real cause. You mentioned that rugby was really important to you (close to life and death importance). Although it's great to care about your game and although it's important to be a good pro, the flip side of the coin is that we can care too much. If rugby is your life and rugby is not going well, it affects everything. It means that your life will not go well. That's a fragile place to be. Our job is to make sure that rugby is just a *part* of your life, and that there is plenty of other important stuff in there as well. You are not just a rugby player. As a person, you are far more than that. Sometimes we forget that we are more than our job. Many players will just see themselves as an athlete and forget the rest. If you can be happy with yourself, and happy with life, you're in a much stronger position. If you have a dip in form or make mistakes, you are much more likely to just let it go. It doesn't make you any less of a professional because you will always work hard on your game. It simply makes you a more rounded and balanced individual.
>   Have fun at the weekend because that's what it's all about. If it's not enjoyable, we ought to ditch it and find something that is fun. To be fair, there can't be many things more enjoyable than playing rugby for a living.

Similar issues immerged when I worked with an elite junior squash player who was struggling to play her best game in the big competitions.

We started by chatting about how you began playing squash. You mentioned that your Dad was a pro and that you started by just playing around with a racket when you were about six years old. It sounds like squash was just something you did for fun because you were around the club a lot. When you were 12 years old you started to compete and you started to enjoy winning as well. I was never a great athlete, but I'm often told it is a nice feeling to win and get that feeling of being the best. It's important to understand that, although this is fine, it brings in another dimension to the game. Squash becomes more than just a way of enjoying yourself and having fun. It becomes important to win because it gives you recognition and respect from other people. Sometimes that becomes the focus – which can become a problem. If you are focusing on being successful because of the recognition, you've made squash more complicated. All of a sudden there is a new agenda that interferes with your ability to 'just play'.

Socrates is famous for extolling the virtues of self-knowledge (Corlett, 1996). He says that knowing yourself is the most vital knowledge we can possibly attain. If you don't know yourself, how can you be yourself? If we are not ourselves, we are never going to achieve our potential (Csikszentmihalyi, 1990). Many athletes and players struggle to perform under pressure because they are conscious of what other people think or expect. In our society, many people live life in an emotional straightjacket because they are worried about what other people think, or what they might say.

If we know ourselves, and are genuinely happy with ourselves, we tend to be less concerned about the outcome, or what other people think of us.

If we have a solid sense of self-worth, we don't need the validation.

If we are sure of ourselves, other people's opinions have less impact.

When we are sure of our self and our skills, we are free to trust our self to perform.

When we trust, we think less and are able to *just play*.

In this mindless (non-thinking) state, we tend to perform more freely.

We become immersed into the activity and operate in the moment.

When all these elements come together, we stand a very good chance of finding 'the zone' and staying there.

These principles underpin peak performances. They are not modern. They have always been a part of human life and human performance. Recently researchers have started to document and study them (Young & Pain, 1999). As human beings we tend to research things we see, create models and theories to explain them, and then try to apply these back to practice. Therefore, coaching methods have been developed around some of these principles during the last 50 years or so (Gallwey, 1986). Some of these theories focus on coaching and learning (Robinson, 2006). Some focus on the psychology of peak performances (Jackson & Csikszentmihalyi, 1999). At their heart, most do not aim to add new techniques or skills. Instead, they aim to remove the inhibitions that stop people from performing naturally. We will explore these over the course of the coming chapters.

Once we can take control, we can genuinely start to produce optimal performances consistently. With this in mind, there are a host of conditions that need to be right for us to continually achieve a peak performance. Some of these require us to take a deep look at ourselves and make some significant shifts in thinking. I can't do that for you, but through the rest of this book I will do my best to lead you through the questions and challenges that make up the journey.

In summary ...

- 'The zone' is a state of complete focus, immersion and absorption in the task.
- We need to focus not only on what we do, but also how we do it.
- There are some key ingredients; clear focus, a love for what you do, confidence, excitement and a good mood.
- We also need to strike a balance between the challenge and our skills.
- Most importantly, we need to be ourselves.

References

Berkow, R. (1984) *The Merck Manual of Diagnosis and Therapy, 15th Edition*, New York: Merck Sharp Publishing.

Corlett, J. (1996) 'Sophistry, Socrates and sport psychology', *The Sport Psychologist*, 10(1), 84–94.

Csikszentmihalyi, M. (1990). *Flow: The Psychology of Optimal Experience*, New York: Harper and Row.

Csikszentmihalyi, M. (2008) 'Creativity, fulfillment and flow', *Keynote Presentation to TED Conference*. 24th October 2008. Online. Available www.youtube.com/watch?v=fXIeFJCqsPs (accessed 15th December 2010).

Flegal, K. and Anderson, M. (2008) 'Overthinking skilled motor performance', *Psychonomic Bulletin & Review*, 15, 927–932.

Frankl, V.E. (1959/1984) *Man's Search for Meaning*, New York: Touchstone.

Gallwey, T. (1986) *The Inner Game of Tennis*, London: Pan Books.

Gallwey, T. (2003) *The Inner Game of Work*, New York: Texere Publishing.

Hartley, S.R. (2012) *How to Shine: Insights Into Unlocking Your Potential from Proven Winners*, Chichester: Capstone.

Jackson, S. and Csikszentmihalyi, M. (1999) *Flow in Sports*, Champaign, IL: Human Kinetics.

Metzinger, T. (2010) *The Ego Tunnel: The Science of the Mind and the Myth of the Self*, New York: Basic Books.

Murphy, S. (1996) *The Achievement Zone*, New York: Berkley.

Nesti, M.S. (2004) *Existential Psychology and Sport: Theory and Application*, Oxford: Routledge.

Nideffer, R.M. (2007) Reliability and Validity of The Attentional and Interpersonal Style Inventory (TAIS) Concentration Scales. In Smith, D. and Bar-Eli, M. *Essential Readings in Sport and Exercise Psychology*, Champaign, IL: Human Kinetics.

Pureakero (2008) Commenting on Csikszentmihalyi, M. (2008) 'Creativity, fulfillment and flow', *Keynote Presentation to TED Conference*. 24th October 2008. Online. Available www.youtube.com/watch?v=fXIeFJCqsPs (accessed 15th December 2010).

Robinson, K. (2006) 'Do schools kill creativity?' *Keynote Presentation to TED Conference*. 26th June 2006. Online. Available www.ted.com/talks/ken_robinson_says_schools_kill_creativity.html> (accessed 15th December 2010).

Seligman, M.E.P. (2005) *Authentic Happiness: Using the New Positive Psychology to Realize Your Potential for Lasting Fulfillment*, New York: Free Press.

Young, J.A. and Pain, M.D. (1999) 'The Zone: Evidence of a universal phenomenon for athletes across sports', *Athletic Insight*, 1(3), 21–30.

The Positive and Negative Spirals

2

I often describe how our mental game works in spirals. There is a positive and negative spiral. I often draw them out as a model to show how all of the components, particularly focus, confidence and motivation, are interdependent. It explains how they underpin and feed each other. It also demonstrates how each spiral is self-perpetuating and compounds.

At this point, I could throw a load of research and theory at you to justify the model. But I'm not going to. There's another form of evidence that is potentially far more powerful.

Your own experience!

Take a look at the spirals.

Match them up against your own lived experience.

Do you recognize them?

Do they reflect how your own mental game works?

Here's the positive spiral.

As you'll see, the base of the spiral has three key ingredients – focus, confidence and motivation. The foundation of the whole thing is focus. More specifically, we start to build the spiral when we're focused on the right thing at the right time.

When we have a simple, clear job, we have a very good chance of doing that job well (Baumeister & Showers, 1986; Donnelly & Ivancevich, 1975). Obviously, we need to have the knowledge, skills, resources and desire to do it as well. But, having a simple, clear task initially gives us a massive advantage. Evidence for this concept comes from a variety of sources – not just sport. Researchers in management settings have identified that both task clarity (Lindsley, Brass & Thomas, 1995) and role clarity (Bray & Brawley, 2002a, 2002b) have a significant impact on performance.

DOI: 10.4324/9781003181491-3

Figure 2.1 The Positive Spiral.

When we understand the job, we're able to do it well. When we do the job well, we normally get a sense of belief, satisfaction and fulfillment. Typically, as human beings, we like exhibiting mastery, and we like to be successful in the things we do. So, when we perform well at something, we tend to want to do it again (Kloosterman, 1988). Psychologists, such as Albert Bandura (1997) have identified strong links between mastery, confidence, achievement and motivation.

These links set up our positive spiral.

When I *focus* on a simple, clear job, I can perform really well in that moment.

When I perform well moment after moment after moment, I build up a bank of evidence that tells me I'm good. This gives me *confidence*.

When I am confident doing something, I want to go and do it again. This fuels my *motivation*.

And, when we're confident and motivated, we're far more likely to step beyond our comfort zone, try new things and fully commit without the concern that we might look stupid if we fail (which I often describe as "releasing our mental hand brake"). When we do all of this, we take a very different view of 'pressure' and start to ask, "What pressure?"

(We'll explore all of these elements in much more detail during the next few chapters.)

These statements may seem perfectly obvious, but their significance is often overlooked. I've seen some highly qualified managers who have missed the importance of these fundamental principles. Consequently, they wonder why their people seem unmotivated, or devoid of confidence. They get frustrated because their people avoid particular tasks or give up too easily, without looking for the reason why.

Think about those tasks that you always seem to avoid, put off or give up on. Are they the ones you'd consider easy and straightforward? Are they tasks that you're confident in, or the ones you're not sure about? Do they tend to be things you're familiar with, or the ones outside your comfort zone?

The positive spiral that we've described also shows us how we can turn around underperformance. It tells us that focus is often the best start point. Most people would probably think that a lack of confidence might best be addressed head on. I have seen many football managers and coaches who believe that a pep talk is a good solution to a team's lack of confidence. I guess many people believe that giving someone a pep talk or some positive feedback will boost their confidence. Equally, many people would probably think that an inspirational speech or a set of attractive incentives would boost motivation. However, they don't often have that effect. It works in the movies. Those famous speeches in films such as *Independence Day* and *Any Given Sunday* are iconic. However, in my experience, it doesn't often work the same way in practice and rarely has a significant and sustained effect on performance. In fact, research also indicates that verbal encouragement is often not enough to increase confidence or turn around a deteriorating performance (Lindsley, et al., 1995).

At the start of the chapter, I also mentioned there was a negative spiral.

As you can see, this spiral starts when we're not focused on the right thing at the right time. When that happens, we tend to make mistakes. Most people don't like making mistakes, so they try to make up for them or rectify them. In doing so, they overanalyze. They beat themselves up. Then they overthink their performance, try too hard and force things. They often become obsessed with the outcome and take their eye off the process. As a result,

Figure 2.2 The Negative Spiral.

they're focused on completely the wrong things, so they make an even bigger mistake.

As you can imagine, it doesn't take long for this spiral to compound. In some cases, people get so far down it they lose their self-belief and motivation. Even professional athletes wonder whether they're capable of performing simple skills.

So, how do we avoid the negative spiral and build the positive spiral?

The simple answer is that we start by focusing on the right thing at the right time. It's one of those 'easier said than done' things. To do it, we also need to realize that focus follows interest, and interest follows what we care most about. Therefore, we need to get our "why" right.

Here's how it works.

I start by simplifying the job. Cut out the complexity and start with a straightforward task that is entirely under our control (Horn, 2008). In a team environment, this means that everyone needs to have a simple job. They have to know what they need to do and how to do it. As a leader, that is arguably our first job (Key, 2006).

Here is an example from an Equestrian rider I worked with a few years ago.

It's two weeks until the competition, which is obviously your big focus at the moment. It's probably fair to say that it is not just a big focus because it's in two weeks' time. It also represents your big ambition in the sport at this point and has been a focus for years. We discussed how you're feeling about it. Your words were 'scared, nervous and worried'. You also talked about the 'pressure of competing for this team in this competition'. We spent quite a while chatting about where this stems from. You talked about missing a big opportunity a few years ago. You also talked about the time and money invested into training and competition. You mentioned the pressure that you have perceived when competing for the team because there are people watching etc. They are all common reasons why people feel nervous before events. In reality, what people do is they tend to attach a lot of meaning to an event, which acts as baggage and forms an agenda that is not really there.

As we continued to chat, we started to become aware of the even bigger issues that have been playing out. You mentioned that typically, you have not been confident in yourself. This has manifested in your work and life. If we're not confident in life, we tend to pin all of our self-worth on the results we get from sport. In a sense, we look to our sporting success or failure to tell us how good we are at life. In this situation we rely on results to feel good about ourselves. This places massive pressure on the performance.

As I said, I believe that there is no such thing as pressure. It is created by our imagination. It has to be imaginary because it is related to a future event. The only place it can exist is our imagination. And, because we create it, we can also get rid of it!

Ultimately, you will feel less pressure to perform in competition when you start to see it for what is really is – just you, the horse and some fences. The job is very simple when you look at it – jump over as many fences as you can as quickly as you can. If it starts to become more than that, we get into problems. The reality is that the job doesn't change just because it's a major competition. It wouldn't change if we put you in an arena with a hundred TV cameras and called it an Olympic final or if it was a training session in your own paddock.

We talked about how you can build your confidence and become happy competing. As you said, priority number one is to have fun and enjoy it – that's the whole point in riding!! We also talked about how your performance is dependent upon your focus. If you are thinking, 'Oh shit, I hope I don't hit the fence', you're more likely to hit it. If you are thinking, 'Don't think about the blue pen', your mind is fixed on the blue pen. The only way to turn this around is to start focusing on the things that will help you perform. As we chatted about it, you mentioned that focusing on the sound of the horses' hooves would be effective. If you can really immerse yourself in that sort of focus, your performance will start to take care of itself.

You also know that you can perform well. You have performed well recently (within the last couple of weeks) and cleared fences that probably you wouldn't have imagined you could clear. Your confidence is built upon evidence. Evidence tells you that you can clear the fences because you do it in training. However, the evidence alone is not enough. You have to recognize it too.

If you can make training as challenging as competition, you will find it easier to see competition the same way that you see training. Train like you compete and compete like you train!

In order to start turning their performance around, most people need a very simple start point. They may see their task as bewildering, maybe even impossible. This is normally a result of getting the job wrong in the first place. We will explore this in much greater detail in Chapter 3. Simply understanding that our clarity of focus often underpins our confidence is the starting point. Understanding that our confidence often underpins our motivation is the next stage.

Here is another example from a Martial Artist who was frustrated by his recent slump in form.

> In order to help you to break the pattern that you are in, I asked you about the mental baggage that you're carrying at the moment. We started this by talking about why it is important to win. You said that winning was important because it tells you that you've done what you're capable of. This is important because you know that your training is coming together and you're heading in the right direction. I asked what the right direction is. You said, 'becoming the British Champ'. I also asked why it's important to become the British Champ. You said that it proves to yourself and everyone else that you can do it. We started to talk about 'everyone else'. You started to tell me about your mates and the blokes at the gym. You also said that until you were 22 years old you were bullied and that being a martial arts champion would help you to counter that.
>
> The problem is that it creates false pressure. It acts like a sack of bricks on your back, weighing you down. It clutters your mind and creates too much 'noise'. It stops you from doing the very simple job – fighting the best fight you can.
>
> Fighting the best fight you can on the day, is your *only* job. The job is not to win. It is not to qualify for anything. It is not to impress anyone or make anyone else happy or proud. It's not to right the wrongs of your past.
>
> Stick to a very simple, clear focus. We chatted briefly about the best point of focus for you. I asked you, 'What is the single most important thing you need to focus on when you're fighting?'
>
> You said – watch the opponent's eyes.
>
> Keep it simple, watch the opponent's eyes and let your instinct and skills do the rest.

Our next step is also to look in detail at how we sharpen focus, control our point of focus and ensure that we're focusing on the most effective things.

In summary ...

- Focus, confidence and motivation are all fundamental to peak performance.
- They are interdependent. They require each other.
- Focus underpins confidence.
- Confidence underpins motivation.
- To turn around a performance, it is often wise to start by clarifying our focus.

References

Bandura, A. (1997) *Self-efficacy: The exercise of control*, New York: Worth Publishers.

Baumeister, R.F. and Showers, C.J. (1986) 'A review of paradoxical performance effects: Choking under pressure in sports and mental tests', *European Journal of Social Psychology*, 16(4), 361–383.

Bray, S.R. and Brawley, L.R. (2002a) 'Role efficacy, role clarity and role performance effectiveness', *Small Group Research*, 33(2), 233–253.

Bray, S.R. and Brawley, L.R. (2002b) 'Efficacy for independent role functions: Evidence from the sport domain, *Small Group Research*, 33(6), 644–666.

Donnelly, J.H. and Ivancevich, J.M. (1975) 'Role clarity and the salesman', *Journal of Marketing*, 39(1), 71–74.

Horn, T. (2008) *Advances in Sport Psychology*, Champaign, IL: Human Kinetics.

Key, A. (2006) 'Knowing your role in rugby', *Rugby Football Union Technical Journal*. 1–6.

Kloosterman, P. (1988) 'Self confidence and motivation in mathematics', *Journal of Educational Psychology*, 80(3), 345–351.

Lindsley, D.H., Brass, D.J. and Thomas, J.B. (1995) 'Efficacy-performance spirals: A multi-level perspective', *Academy of Management Review*, 20(3), 645–678.

Hone Your Focus $\qquad$ **3**

DOI: 10.4324/9781003181491-4

"Progress has little to do with speed, but much to do with direction".

Anon

What is it that makes the difference between the true greats and the 'also-rans'? Is it talent? Is it determination and drive? Is it attitude? In reality it is probably a combination of all of these and more. Over the years I have been worked with a lot of athletes, from those at the very pinnacle of their sport, to junior athletes learning the ropes. No matter what level, there is something that successful athletes have in common – their ability to focus!

True champions show an incredible level of long-term focus (Jones & Moorhouse, 2007). They work consistently for years and years to perfect their performance. Many world class athletes didn't have exceptional natural talent in their younger years. If you look at their ability alone, they probably wouldn't stand out. But there are likely to be clues that they are champions in the making. Day on day they will practice a little longer, work a little harder and push themselves further (Colvin, 2008). They will be incredibly focused on their sport and dedicate themselves to refining the tiny details, every day for years. If they become 0.1 percent better than their opposition each day, it won't take long before there is a noticeable gap. This relentless long-term focus starts to create champions (England & Wales Cricket Board, 2005).

It is long-term focus that Olympians require to drive them through multiple four-year preparation cycles (Johnson, 1996). They can go months without a major competition, so they need incredible focus to keep training to the highest level. However, it's not just Olympians that need long-term focus. It is easy for a professional athlete to get lost in a busy season. One week can blend into the next. Professional players can slip into a cycle of mindless training. If they're not careful, they end up going through the motions and simply repeating the cycle without really driving their improvement.

Obviously, this is not just true in sports. It applies equally to all areas of life. In reality, very few people actually improve their performance day on day. When I wrote *How to Shine*, I discovered that world class performers often subscribe to a very simple philosophy.

Better today than yesterday.

Better tomorrow than today.

And, while it sounds obvious, it's extremely rare! (Hartley, 2012).

We know it is not possible to develop excellence in anything overnight. True success takes a great deal of time, effort and investment, consistently delivered over a long period. In many cases, there is a guiding vision behind it all – someone's dream. Examples can be seen in biographies of business founders, such as Fred Smith the founder of FedEx (Trimble, 1993).

If you listen to interviews with athletes just after they win medals, many will say that "it is a dream come true". They've probably been imagining that moment since childhood. Their dream has been fueling their motivation, which gets them out of bed at a ridiculous time of the morning for years on end (Torres and Weil, 2009). It keeps them going when they're in pain and pushes them through their dark times. Perhaps, more importantly, it also helps them focus on what they need to do every day, to achieve that dream.

"I dream my painting and then I paint my dream", Vincent Van Gogh.

Having a dream or a vision is great. However, we need to know how to turn that dream into a tangible reality. We have to know exactly what we need to do today and tomorrow, in order to get us close to achieving the dream. If we simply keep dreaming, we will just be a dreamer. We need to *do*, in order to achieve.

Many people have a real challenge converting their dream or their vision into reality. The challenge lies in the fact that the dream or vision is often an outcome. It is often a result. For example, a football manager dreams of winning the Champions League, an athlete dreams of Olympic Gold, an entrepreneur dreams of having a multi-billion-pound business empire. They are all outcomes. Although the outcome may be our driver and our motivator, focusing on it may actually be counterproductive. If we focus on the outcome, we often fail to focus on the things we need to do to achieve it. By focusing on the outcome, we often forget to focus on the processes that will get us there. This principle underpins business improvement models such as Six Sigma (Keller, 2009) and Kaizen (Imai, 1986).

Focus comes when we simplify and clarify.

I worked with a swimmer for around eight years. When we started working together, he was a decent national standard athlete who had just competed at the World Student Games but had not yet won a full Great Britain cap. He dreamed of winning Olympic Gold in his favored event; the 100m breaststroke. For the first three years or so we worked in a slight fog. We were making progress to a certain extent but, to be honest, our strategy was a 'best guess'. We were a little bit reactionary. It almost felt like we were navigating in very poor visibility and were reacting as things appeared. At the time, we were working to a set of goals which included 'making the GB team', 'securing funding', 'securing sponsorship', 'qualifying for championships', 'winning key races' etc. After about three years, we came to a stark realization. To that point we had made a fundamental error. We had got the job wrong. His job was not to make the GB team. It wasn't to secure funding or sponsorship. It wasn't to qualify for championships or win races.

He was a 100m swimmer in a 50m pool. His job was very, very simple. The job was to swim two lengths of the pool as quickly as he could.

That realization was like a blinding flash of light. It made an enormous impact on how we worked, our effectiveness and our end results. Immediately we started to identify exactly what he needed to do, in order to swim two lengths of the pool as quickly as he could. He pulled together a team of specialists including his coach, physiotherapist, biomechanist, performance analyst, nutritionist, physiologist, strength and conditioning coach and performance-lifestyle adviser. Everyone was challenged to help him swim two lengths of the pool as quickly as he possibly could.

We broke down his stroke. We analyzed his technique. He started to figure out what the key elements of his performance were and put programs in place to improve them. He changed his training regime to take out many of the things he habitually did (because they had always been on the program) and replaced them with things that would contribute to swimming two lengths quicker. In came yoga, gymnastics and specialist physiotherapy work to improve his streamlining. Out went some of the swim sessions and strength sessions that may not have been contributing. We spent two to three years working on a project to help improve his starts by a few tenths of a second and another to work on his turns. We analyzed his performances to find the perfect race strategy for him and then put a program in place to practice and perfect it.

His whole outlook changed once we figured out what his real job was. It became a benchmark and a filter. Before doing anything, he would ask, "Will this help me swim two lengths of the pool quicker?" If it would make him quicker, he'd consider doing it. If not, it would be binned. We also started asking whether it was likely to knock a whole second off his time or 0.000001 seconds off. Obviously, the things which make the biggest impact had a higher priority.

This thought process set up our working practice for the last four or five years of his career. It helped him to become infinitely more focused, more effective and more successful. Because he swam two lengths of the pool more quickly, he won more races, became a regular on the British team (and in fact became British number one for several years), he qualified for major championships, made finals at World Championships, Olympic Games and won two gold medals at the Commonwealth Games. He finished his career as the seventh fastest person in history in his event (Hartley, 2013).

This all probably seems blatantly obvious to you. Why hadn't we thought of this sooner?

Well, I'm certainly not claiming to be particularly clever. We probably should have realized it a lot earlier. However, most people rarely stop and think about what their job really is. Many of us know our dream. We have the vision. However, most people do what Chris and I did for the first three years. We just followed the daily pattern. Like most athletes, he did what it said on the schedule. I guess it becomes habit and to a certain extent you accept it and just fall into the pattern. We may not stop and actually check that everything we are doing is actually taking us towards our dream via the most effective possible route. Therefore, there is a gap between what we are doing right now and our dream.

In recent years, I have started to apply these principles to my performance coaching work outside of sport. I know the enormous positive impact it had when we discovered Chris's 'Two Lengths of the Pool'. Therefore, I now encourage everyone to understand their own 'Two Lengths'.

What is your Two Lengths of the Pool?
What is your job in the simplest possible terms?

Here are a few examples that have come from applying this exercise to both groups and individuals.

100m breaststroke swimmer in a 50m pool

'Swim two lengths of the pool as quickly as I can'.

Olympic Archer

'Get as many of my arrows as close to the center of the target as I can'.

A Soccer Team

'To score as many goals as possible and to concede as few as possible'.

Bakery

'To sell as many exceptional quality bakery products as possible, profitably'.

An Insurance Sales Team

'Generate high-quality leads and convert them to repeating sales'.

Managing Partner of a Law Firm

'Create the strategy and structure to grow the business, profitably'.

Business Development Director of the same Law Firm

'Maximize the income of the business through selling legal services'.

You may have noticed that there is a theme to many of these. There is a set of guidelines that they all conform to.

1. It needs to be a process, not an outcome.
2. It has to be entirely within your control.
3. It should really fit neatly behind the words ..'My/our job is to ..'
4. It needs to be very specific.
5. We need to know that if we achieve the 'Two Lengths', we've accomplished the job completely.

Let's take a look at Chris's definition again in more detail. His job is to ...

• Swim
  Not run, walk, cycle, canoe or propel himself by any other means.
• Two lengths of the pool
  He's not particularly bothered whether he reaches the 50m first, and he doesn't need to be able to do miles in the pool either.

- as quickly

  he is measured by time, not profit or distance or any other marker.
- as he can

  He is not trying to swim quicker than everyone else, because that's not within his control. He has not set a target (i.e., in under 60s), because that's also pretty arbitrary. If he swam under 60 seconds but it wasn't the fastest he could swim, he will not have produced his best. If he swims the fastest he possibly can and it's 60.1 seconds, he couldn't swim any quicker. His job is to swim as fast as he can on the day. And he'll work to be quicker today than he was yesterday, and quicker tomorrow than he is today.

Once you've found your Two Lengths, stress test it to make sure it's robust and it stands up to challenge. Make sure that it really is your job and that by delivering it, you will ultimately be successful. For example, if your Two Lengths is related to business performance, it should probably make some reference to profit. In business, if you are not profitable, you won't be around long. Equally, for charities, operating within budget should arguably be in the Two Lengths somewhere. If not, you're not going to be operating very long either.

Fred Smith, founder of FedEx often refers to the *one thing*, that the business is there to do. He advocates knowing the *one thing*, and sticking to it (Trimble, 1993).

So, once you've found your Two Lengths, what is the next step?

The next step is to look at *how* you deliver it. In my work, I ask clients to identify the five most important and significant factors that will help them deliver their Two Lengths. If they could only have a list of five, what would those five be? Because I'm a sport psychology consultant and performance coach, I decided to give these five things a snazzy title ... the Five Keys.

There is a good reason why I ask for a maximum of five. We can just about focus on five things, but we'd struggle to really deliver against more than five. We'd get a law of diminishing returns, and we wouldn't really do them justice if we tried to address more than five. If we have less than five, that's okay. A list of three is fine by me. The problem comes when we have too many things. Our brain simply can't do it (Richtel, 2010).

Often, just simplifying the job helps us to be successful (Trout & Rivkin, 1998).

I worked with one of our Olympic squads just after they returned from the Beijing Games in 2008. They had a disappointing Games and had returned empty-handed. It was slightly unexpected because their previous Olympic performance was pretty good. The athletes were very capable, and they had one of the world's most respected coaches. In one of our first meetings, I asked the coach to list the five most significant factors that would impact on the athletes' performance.

"What are the five things that they really need to do when they're standing on the line, ready to shoot? If they could only do five things, which would be the most crucial five?"

As I asked the coach the question, he looked at me perplexed. He then proceeded to draw up a list of 32 crucial factors that each athlete should be focused on when standing on the line ready to shoot. All of a sudden it became clear to me why these athletes had not performed. The greatest mind on the planet could not focus on getting 32 things right all at once. As I challenged him to reduce the list, he became adamant that you could not prioritize just five. In talking to the athletes, it became obvious that they were very unclear about what they needed to do to perform well. When they stood on the line, their mind was whirring with the long list of things they needed to do. As a result, they underperformed and became confused, frustrated and disillusioned. A skill that had once been second nature to them had become complicated and difficult.

Have a look at your Two Lengths. What are your *Five Keys*? What are the five things, which if you do them well, will almost guarantee you success? They have to be the five most significant factors – the five which will have the greatest impact on your performance and that will deliver your Two Lengths. It's worth spending time to ensure that you are happy with your Five Keys. When we get the process right, we should be able to apply almost all of our focus to these keys. If we deliver these five to the best of our ability, we will almost certainly deliver our Two Lengths. And, if we have our Two Lengths right, we know that we will be successful when we deliver it.

Once you know these five, you have a very effective set of things to focus on. The next stage of the challenge is to control your focus on the things that will give you your best performance.

So, how do you control focus?

When I work with athletes, I often describe focus as a torch beam (Taylor, 2010; Taylor & Wilson, 2005). The torch beam only focuses on one thing at a time. Our focus works in the same way. If we think we're focusing on lots of things at once, or multi-tasking, our focus is hopping between a myriad of different things. It only settles on any one of them for a split second before dashing off to the next (Hamilton, 2008; Weissman, Roberts, Visscher, & Woldorff, 2006).

The challenge for many athletes is actually to take control of the torch and decide where the beam will shine. What is it that you need to focus on? How can you direct your beam and keep it steady? It's tough to do at times. A lot of us don't have the mental discipline required to hold our focus for any prolonged period. We are easily distracted and find that something draws the torch beam. This tends to be exacerbated if we're scared (Horn, 2008).

Imagine walking along a path in the dark with a narrow torch beam. If you are scared, you react differently. If you hear something go bump behind you, the likelihood is that you'll spin round and shine your torch on it to see what made the noise. This draws your beam from the path you are supposed to be following. If you were comfortable walking the path, or you could see pretty clearly, you would be much less likely to take your beam off the path.

One of the greatest sources of distraction, is our own thoughts!

In sport, if we're not feeling confident, we tend to start overthinking (Rotella, 2005). This draws our focus (Blanke, 2007). A tennis player should arguably be 100 percent focused on the ball. If she's not focused on the ball, the chances of playing a decent shot are pretty remote. If the player is thinking about the mistake she made in her last shot (instead of shining her torch on the ball) the beam will be focused on her own thoughts.

When we overthink, we experience what I call 'thought blindness'. Imagine a batsman in cricket facing a 90 mph delivery. The batsman has to select a shot and execute it in a split second (Cork, Justham & West, 2008). Thinking takes a relatively long time. If the batsman thinks, he will not see the bowler or the ball clearly because his brain will be tied up with his thoughts. As a result, his brain will not register what his eyes are seeing. The only way for the batsman to play a good shot, is to simply watch the bowler and the ball as closely as possible and let his unconscious mind play the shot. The batsman has to be in a 'mindless' state (Rotella, 2005).

Many players do need to think at times. They may need to decide where to play shots and how to play their game tactically. However, when it comes to executing the shot, thinking tends to interfere (Gallwey, 1986). Our 'non-thinking', unconscious mind controls our movement. If we want to play great shots, we have to feel the shots, see the shots and hear the shots. We can't think them. To be in 'the zone' we need to be totally absorbed in what we're doing, to the exclusion of everything else. The more intensely we can immerse ourselves in the shot, the greater our chances of entering 'the zone'. When we engage our senses fully, we will start to immerse ourselves and become absorbed in the shots. In order to do this, we need to be able to control our focus (Csikszentmihalyi, 1990).

For years I have heard people ask, 'How do I stop thinking negative thoughts?' The answer is alarmingly simple. Focus on something else. If you try not to think about something, the chances are you will think about it even more. Here's a challenge. Don't think about the word *blue*. Don't think about *the color blue*. Don't think about *blue* things. Think about anything except BLUE.

What are you thinking?

One way way to stop thinking about blue is to start focusing on RED. Red roses ... red Ferraris ... red anything. The same is true of negative thoughts. The way to stop thinking them is to start focusing on something else (Hartley, 2022). You do this naturally when you're confident. That's why you play better when you're confident. Confidence and focus are closely linked. If you can control confidence, focus will automatically become easier. But the start point for many is to control our focus. Choose to focus on something that will help you play better (Anderson, 2000). Arguably the best way to focus on our performance is to engage our senses (Gallwey, 1986; Cook, 2005; Rauch, 2010; McKim, 1980), particularly your three primary senses in sport. Focus on what you see, hear and feel.

Here are some very personal examples from athletes.

Martial Artist

• Watch the opponent's eyes.

International Squash Players

• Watch the movement on the ball.
• Feel the shots.
• Hear the sound that your shots are making or the sound of your footwork.

Hammer Thrower

• Feel the balance in your feet.
• Hear the sound of your rhythm.
• Feel the smoothness in your movement.

Tennis Player

• Watch the ball and pick it up as early as possible (as your opponent plays the shot, rather than as the ball comes over the net).
• Feel 'lightness' in your feet and hear the sound of your footwork.

Golfer

- Hear the sound of the club hitting the ball.
- Feel your balanced start position.
- Close your eyes to stop yourself following the ball.

Javelin Thrower

- Feel the solidity of the front leg (and knee).
- Hear the sound of the rhythm in the approach run.

These are the points of focus which the athletes felt would give them the best performance. It's important to focus rather than think. We need to notice, rather than analyze. It's easy to start analyzing how something feels. If we do this, we could start screwing up our technique because our thinking brain starts to try to control our movement. Noticing allows us to simply observe and be aware of these sensory cues, without feeling the need to control or change them. Our subconscious mind will execute the skills. We simply need to see, hear, feel and trust! (Gallwey, 1986).

The same principles apply outside of sport. Although we may not have the same need to see, hear and feel a performance, we will need to focus on the Five Key things that will ensure we deliver our own 'Two Lengths of the Pool'. We need to keep our focus on the processes and make sure we deliver those. When we consistently deliver the processes, the outcomes will inevitably follow. If not, we probably need to review the Five Keys that we selected.

But how do we keep the torch on those key things?

First, we need to recognize that focus follows interest (Gallwey, 2003). If we're more interested in winning than performing well, this can affect our focus. If we're losing, our torch beam will start to settle on our doubts and negative thoughts. Our mind will be dominated by thoughts such as 'What if I don't win?', or 'I can't see how I'm going to win this'. If we're genuinely more interested in performing well, it is easier to focus on the things that will help us perform well (i.e., what we need to see, hear or feel).

Our interest will also be heightened if we strike the balance between the perceived challenge and our perception of our skills. Mihaly Csikszentmihalyi (1990) found that peak performances (also known as 'flow'), occur when we achieve this balance; in particular, when both the level of challenge and our skills are both high. Put simply, it means that we perform at our best when we're engaged in a challenge that we believe we're capable of, but that pushes us. If we don't have the stimulus from the challenge, it is unlikely to grab our attention. We know this from our own experience. When we are engaged in something challenging, we need to give it our full attention and we tend to become immersed in the task. This will only remain as long as we can engage with the task successfully. If the task is not challenging enough, we get bored. If our skills are not up to the challenge, then we'll quickly get frustrated and lose interest. If a challenge is far beyond our perceived skills, we might end up becoming anxious.

You can practice controlling your focus and holding your focus on specific cues. Sports players can do this in training. They can select one of their key points of focus and lock onto it. There will be a whole host of things that will try to draw your focus. Some of these will be external (such as the opposition or referee), and some will be internal (such as your own thoughts or doubts). The challenge is to bring your focus back to those highly effective cues as soon as you can. What should you be focusing on? What should you be seeing, hearing or feeling? (Cook, 2005).

Outside of sport, the same principles apply. Often, I challenge people to keep tabs on how much of their time has been spent delivering their Five Keys and their own Two Lengths. Sometimes we use simple exercises to outline the activities they do in the course of their working days. We then categorize these as 'core activities', 'support activities' or 'distractions'. I define 'core' as activities that directly contribute to your Two Lengths. The support activities help you to do the core activities better, although they may not in themselves be classed as 'core'. Finally, 'distractions' do not contribute to the Two Lengths and actually may detract from it. In addition to knowing which activities fall into each category, we can also estimate how much time, energy and focus goes into each. This gives us a simple means of assessing effectiveness.

Focus is the cornerstone of our performance. We need to have a simple, clear focus first. If we have a simple, clear focus, we're likely to be able to perform. Once we perform well, we will become more confident. When we're confident, we are likely to be motivated to do it again. Performance starts with simplicity and clarity.

In summary ...

- Focus is the foundation. Simplify and clarify!
- Focus on the processes.
- Find your 'Two Lengths' and 'Five Keys'.
- Focus is like a torch beam.
- Identify the most effective processes to focus on, and hone in.
- If you want to stop thinking about X, start focusing on Y.
- Focus through your senses; see, hear and feel the performance.

References

Anderson, M. (2000) *Doing Sport Psychology*, Champaign, IL: Human Kinetics.

Blanke, G. (2007) 'How to stop overthinking your life and start living', *Real Simple*, August 2007.

Colvin, G. (2008) *Talent is Overrated: What Really Separates World Class Performers From Everybody Else*, New York: Portfolio.

Cook, M. (2005) *The FreeFlow Method*, Northumberland, UK: SportsCoach21.

Cork, A., Justham, L. and West, A. (2008) 'Cricket batting: Stroke timing of a batsman when facing a bowler and a bowling machine (P26)', *The Engineering of Sport*, 7, 143–150.

Csikszentmihalyi, M. (1990) *Flow: The Psychology of Optimal Experience*, New York: Harper and Row.

England & Wales Cricket Board (2005) *Planning for Long Term Success*, London. England & Wales Cricket Board.

Gallwey, T. (1986) *The Inner Game of Tennis*, London: Pan Books.

Gallwey, T. (2003) *The Inner Game of Work*, New York: Texere Publishing.

Hamilton, J. (2008) 'Think you're multi-tasking? Think again', *NRP*. 2nd October 2008.

Hartley, S.R. (2012) *How to Shine: Insights Into Unlocking Your Potential from Proven Winners*, Chichester: Capstone.

Hartley, S.R. (2013) *Two Lengths of the Pool: Sometimes the Simplest Ideas Have the Greatest Impact*, Leeds: Be World Class.

Hartley, S.R. (2022) *Silence Your Demons*, Leeds: Be World Class.

Horn, T. (2008) *Advances in Sport Psychology*, Champaign, IL: Human Kinetics.

Imai, M (1986) *Kaizen: The Key to Japan's Competitive Success*, London: McGraw Hill.

Johnson, M. (1996) *Slaying the Dragon: How to Turn Your Small Steps into Great Feats*, New York: HarperCollins.

Jones, G. and Moorhouse, A. (2007) *Developing Mental Toughness*, London: How to Books.

Keller, P. (2009) *The Six Sigma Handbook*, London: McGraw Hill Professional.

McKim, R. (1980) *Experiences in Visual Thinking, 2nd Edition*, California: Brooks / Cole Publishing.

Rauch, S. (2010) 'Trager ®: A body / mind approach in sport psychology', *Podium Sports Journal*, 1st April. Online. Available www.podiumsportsjournal.com/2010/04/01/trager%C2%AE-a-bodymind-approach-in-sports-psychology/ (accessed 15th December 2010).

Richtel, M. (2010) 'Multitasking hurts brain's ability to focus, scientists say', *Seattle Times*, 6th June 2010.

Rotella, R.J. (2005) *Putting Out Of Your Mind*, London: Pocket Books.

Taylor, J. (2010) 'Understanding focus in sports', *Psychology Today*. 13th July 2010. Online. Available www.psychologytoday.com/blog/the-power-prime/201007/sports-understanding-focus-in-sports> (accessed 15th December 2010).

Taylor, J. and Wilson, G.S. (2005) *Applying Sport Psychology: Four Perspectives*, Champaign, IL: Human Kinetics.

Torres, D. and Weil, E. (2009) *Age is just a number: Achieve Your Dreams at Any Age in Your Life*, New York: Crown Archetypes.

Trimble, V. (1993) *Overnight Success: FedEx and Frederick Smith, It's Renegade Creator*, New York: Crown.

Trout, J. and Rivkin, S. (1998) *The Power of Simplicity*, New York: McGraw Hill.

Weissman, D.H., Roberts, K.C., Visscher, K.M. and Woldorff, M.G. (2006) 'The neural bases of momentary lapses in attention', *Nature Neuroscience*, 9, 971–978.

Control Your Confidence   **4**

I worked for a few years in Premier League football. I often heard the manager and coaches saying, "If we could just win a couple of games, we'd get our confidence back and then we'll start playing well". I've been fortunate to have worked in a huge variety of sports during the past 25 years and one thing I've noticed is that confidence is the Holy Grail. Most athletes recognize that when they are confident, they perform well, think less, and play a more natural and normally effortless game. It's equally true outside of sport. I've spoken to numerous sales directors and senior sales managers who have told me, "Sales is 90 percent confidence". However, as those football managers highlighted, finding your confidence is often thought of as a 'chicken and egg thing'. Without the confidence you're unlikely to perform well, but you need a good performance to feel confident … or do you? As a performance coach, I teach people to take control of their confidence.

I recently worked with a sales team who were not performing consistently. When I discussed the issue with the sales executives, many of them described a very simple pattern. When they were selling, they were confident, and they sold more. When they weren't selling, their confidence took a hit and they struggled. I liken this to centre forwards in a football team. When they are scoring, they are confident, and they score more. When their confidence is low, they become 'shot shy' and therefore they don't take as many shots and consequently don't score as many goals. This is a pretty fragile system and one where the performer (the sales executive or the center forward in these examples) is not in control. They are essentially relying on circumstance to provide them with 'a bit of luck'. When our performance is reliant on external factors (other people or circumstances), we are in a position of weakness.

DOI: 10.4324/9781003181491-5

Where does confidence come from? Confidence comes from evidence (Bandura, 1997). The reason that you're confident tying your shoelaces is because you have done it hundreds of times before and been consistently successful. You have the evidence. Most of us would be less confident if we were asked to climb Mount Everest. The simple fact is that we don't have the bank of evidence telling us we've done it successfully many times before. If we take this logic a step further, we also know that even experienced climbers find Everest challenging (Clash, 2003).

What happens if our bank of evidence actually tells us that we've continually tried and failed at something? How confident will we be in our next attempt?

So, what's the solution?

I hear many people trying to boost someone's confidence with a 'pep talk' or by giving positive feedback. In business and sport, managers and coaches will often try to persuade someone that they have the ability. A coach might point towards recent good performances or results. A manager might remind a team member of successes they've had in the past. I have found that this is quite common in sales environments. The aim, of course, is to help the person to see the positive evidence, which will then hopefully increase their confidence. Occasionally it might have an effect. Often the effect will be fairly short-lived and pretty fragile. However, it does highlight an important point. Our confidence comes from the evidence that we *see*. The fact that evidence exists is not enough. We have to see it and recognize it if it is to have an impact and actually build our confidence. Some people appear to be 'naturally confident', whereas others don't. In reality, those who appear naturally confident probably look for and see evidence of their ability. It doesn't mean that they have more ability, but they look for the evidence and therefore see the evidence more readily than others (Branden, 1984; Branden, 2001).

I once worked with a gymnast. She was 16 years old and one of the highest ranked gymnasts in the country. Most people would agree that she was very good. However, she had incredibly low self-confidence. She did not think she was good. In one of our first sessions, I watched her complete an exercise in training. She called the exercise a 'circuit' and she performed it on the beam. The circuit involved five different skills, performed five times each (i.e., 25 discrete skills in total). As I watched, I noticed that she would occasionally stop and make notes. At the end of the circuit, I asked her what she was writing.

"I write down all my mistakes", she replied.

When we evaluated her performance together, there was one imperfection in each of the different skills, but she only produced that imperfection once in the five attempts. Therefore, of the 25 attempts, only five had an imperfection. In reality, 80 percent was perfect. When we discussed the degree of the imperfections, it turned out that the 'imperfect' attempts were probably rated at about 8/10 (i.e., 80 percent correct). The mistakes (as she called them) were certainly not catastrophic. In reality, they were simply not 100 percent perfect. Of all the evidence available, the gymnast was choosing to look at the imperfections. She was only looking at her mistakes. She only saw what she could not do. As a result, her perception was dominated by mistakes and so she concluded that she wasn't any good.

"We see in the world what we look for".

Anon

Knowing this, it is important that we look for solid sources of evidence, on which to build our confidence (Dayton, 2007).

What do you think most people's confidence is underpinned by?

What is your confidence underpinned by?

The answer for most people is 'results'. However, that's not a strong position to be in. If your confidence is reliant upon winning or losing, it is going to be pretty fragile. Winning or losing is something you cannot directly control. There are a huge number of factors that dictate the result. Although you have a certain degree of control, you can't control everything that influences a result. In sport, for example, the referee normally has an enormous impact on results. Do you really want refereeing decisions to influence your confidence? In sales, the customer arguably has the biggest influence. Although a sales executive can do a fantastic job of positioning a product or service, they cannot make the decision for the customer. In the sales scenario there are hundreds of factors outside the sales executive's control that will ultimately influence the decision.

Aside from results, most people's confidence is influenced by a host of other external factors. The more common one is probably other people's feedback.

I worked with a footballer a few years ago who was lacking confidence. We chatted about who and what had the biggest influence. Interestingly, the manager had the biggest influence, followed by other players, the crowd, his dad and even the newspaper report. When we looked at it objectively, it was likely that the manager's feedback was not going to be completely reliable. The manager will be watching 20 plus players on the field and not really focusing on him. If his team wins, the manager is likely to be happy. If they lose, he won't be. That also goes for the other players, the crowd and the newspaper. As we chatted, it became apparent that the player's own views counted for very little. Ironically, of course, the player himself was in the best position to review his game and probably had the most accurate feedback. He'd seen and felt his performance from inside his body. However, he'd given control of his confidence over to everyone else. As a result, his confidence wasn't based on his own performance; it was based on how everyone else felt. That's a vulnerable position to be in.

This example shows that controlling confidence often starts with how we control feedback. Our footballer started to control his confidence when he started to honestly and objectively evaluate his own performances. It sounds pretty simple and straightforward, but let's take a look at that in more detail.

First, he needs to be honest. If he has had a poor game, he needs to be honest about it. Equally, if he has played really well, he needs to be honest rather than modest. Most people struggle with this stage. We are either too harsh on ourselves or look for excuses. This feedback is only for our own benefit. What is the point in being anything other than completely honest? The only one who will suffer the consequences of dishonesty is ourself.

Second, our player needs to be objective. The player needs to use his own evaluation and then integrate feedback from others. The aim is not to be arrogant and ignore the feedback of others. However, we shouldn't rely completely on the feedback from others either. We should have our own view. We need to be able to provide ourselves with objective feedback on a performance. I have worked with a lot of athletes and business people who rely completely on their coach or manager for feedback. Like any state of dependency, it puts us in a potential position of weakness. The strongest position is to use the benefit of both viewpoints and integrate the feedback of others with our own objective views. These views should not be driven by emotion, but by the evidence. We should look at our performance as a whole, not just focus on the two or three things that went either particularly well or badly. Many athletes fall into the trap of thinking the whole performance was horrendous because of one error which cost them the match. In reality, that is not an objective evaluation, it is an emotional reaction. If our feedback is based on a negative emotional reaction, our confidence will probably suffer. We should not ignore the error or pretend that it was okay, but we do need to put it in context with the rest of the performance so that we get a fair and proper view.

Finally, our player needs to evaluate the performance. Most players don't evaluate, they judge. Normally the judgment is emotionally charged and contains little in the way of useful information. How many times have you described a performance as 'good', 'okay' or '****'. None of those judgments have any value. They will not help you become better. They will not improve your performance or help you to engineer your confidence. When I work with athletes, I often start by asking them to rate their performance on a scale of zero to ten. It's never going to be a zero. There will always be something in it that was positive. Equally, it's very rare that a performance would be a 'perfect' (flawless) ten. Whatever you score, there will always be two elements to your score. What did you do well (which stopped you from scoring zero)? What can you improve (which stopped you from scoring ten)? Knowing these two things will help you ensure that your next performance is better than this one.

'But what happens if I scored a two? Surely, I'm not going to be confident going into the next game', I hear you ask.

That depends on how you decide to respond to a 2/10 score. One response would be to feel disheartened and start to convince yourself that you're rubbish. The other response is to identify the things you need to work on, and then do it. Start on the training ground. Start by getting the basics nailed down, and then build and build until you start to become more confident that you can deliver. There is a very simple formula which you can use to create confidence. Build on what you can do!

One spring morning, I sat down with a junior international archer. I asked why she looked troubled. She told me she was dreading school, particularly Business Studies. I challenged her to tell me five questions that she would love to see on the exam paper because she knew the answers inside out. Initially she told me she didn't have any. After a little grouching and muttering she agreed to think about it overnight. Next day she said she had seven questions.

"Great", I said, "Your job now is to research five more questions so that you know them inside out too. You need to know them so well that you'd love to see them on the exam paper. Once you know these five new questions, you'll have 12".

I then asked her how confident she would feel if she had 150 questions that she'd love to see on the exam paper. Of course, she'd feel confident. So, the formula is simple. Once you've got 12, research another five, then another five until you have enough to feel truly confident.

She got a B in her exam – well done Caz!

Here is an excerpt from a report that I wrote for a female junior tennis player following a review session. In the session, she told me that she'd rated one of her performances as a 5/10. Her initial reaction was to become frustrated and lose confidence. However, there is an opportunity to use the performance to increase her confidence by working on the weaknesses until she becomes confident in those areas of her game.

> You said that your opponent served faster and with more spin. She was a left-handed player and served wide. The spin made the ball bounce up in front of you, which caused you a challenge. In addition, she returned deep off of your serve, which also made things more difficult for you.

We talked about how you can change your game to cope with this challenge. I'm a great believer in attacking challenges like this and making sure you can become comfortable with them. The only way to do that is to train these elements of your game. It sounds as if your training partner Jonny can really help challenge you. He is tall, powerful, has a strong left-handed serve and can put spin on the shot. If you knew you could cope with Jonny's serve comfortably, how confident would you feel facing a similar opponent in competition next time? If you use this experience and work on your game, you can actually increase your confidence in the long run.

You can use the same simple principles to control your own confidence. Start with what you're doing well and add to it. Practice the bits you're not as confident in until you know you can do them. I often speak to athletes just before they embark on major competitions. As you can imagine, confidence is often a natural topic of conversation. There are a variety of sources from which elite performers draw their confidence (Hayes, Maynard, Thomas & Bawden, 2007). However, it probably won't come as any great surprise to you that there is a recurring theme with these conversations. When performers feel more prepared, they are likely to be more confident (Horn, 2008; Orlick, 2000). Good preparation gives us the evidence that we can perform well. This is not true only in sports. McDonald, Orlick & Letts (1995) found exactly the same with surgeons. Imagine two scenarios. The first is a scenario in which a swimmer has had an almost perfect training cycle leading up to a major competition. They have been hitting very good times in training and their 'warm up' competitions. They feel strong, fast, lean and powerful. During the cycle they have made some significant technical changes and have started to see a positive impact on their performances. How confident do you think they will feel?

Let's compare that to a swimmer who has been plagued by injury and illness throughout the cycle. They have struggled to get a coherent period of uninterrupted training and don't feel like they have fully tested their body yet. As a result, they haven't been able to enter many of the warm-up competitions and say that they're feeling a little 'race rusty'. How confident are they likely to feel?

I know those two examples are at the opposite ends of the scale. However, this principle applies across the board. Image that one of our athletes has really focused on their training during the last three or four months. They have started to work on the fine details of their technique and have pushed themselves further than ever before in their sessions. In their heart of hearts, they know that the last cycle has been their best yet and that they have made substantial progress as a result. Let's compare them to an athlete who has approached the last three or four months in the same way they have always done. They turn up and follow the session they are given. Normally, if the coach asks for 100 percent they give about 90, and always leave a little in reserve. They also have a tendency to drift off in a session and don't really focus on the details. Although they complete the sessions, they don't get the maximum possible benefit. Some of what they do will be good, but a lot will be sloppy. What impact do you think this will have on the respective athletes' confidence?

I often hear how confident an athlete is when I speak to them. Some athletes will tell me they 'hope' they will perform well. Others will tell me they 'think' they'll perform, or that they 'are confident'. Towards the top end of the scale, there are a few athletes that 'believe' they will perform well. The ultimate expression of confidence is '*knowing*'. However, athletes don't always say, 'I know'. Sometimes they say, 'I hope' or 'I believe'. If we look at the range of possible responses, we can see a confidence scale. At the bottom end we could find, 'I hope', and at the top end, 'I know'.

How confident are you that you will perform well?

I hope – I think – I'm confident – I believe – I know

Those who are underprepared often say, "I hope". Those who are well-prepared and have the evidence to tell them they can perform will often say, "I know". I use this scale with performers in all disciplines. It gives me a start point in understanding their levels of confidence and allows me to explore the issue further.

A while ago, I was asked to work with an International Squash team. As we began the program, it became obvious that they had an issue when they faced the world number one. It was becoming something of a mental block. Our players didn't really believe that they could beat her. The evidence told them that the world number one had only been beaten once or twice in the previous two years. None of our players had beaten her even though they'd produced some of their best performances against her. They described the world number one as possessing some very 'hard to beat' qualities. She was physically fast and powerful, and she hit the ball hard. When one of our players made a shot that would win beat any other opponent, the world number one would return it. They likened the experience to playing against a top male player.

We needed to give our team evidence which proved that they could beat the world number one. Therefore, we deliberately created situations where our players faced fast, hard-hitting opponents. We started in the spring, matching the England women's team against 18-19-year-old elite male players. The young male players were fast, powerful and hard-hitting. Over the period of six months or so, the women played regularly against fast, powerful players. They naturally started to increase the pace of their game and became accustomed to playing fast-paced opponents. They started to develop tactics and approaches which gave them the upper hand and disarmed their opponent. In the first 'test match' between our team and the elite U19 men, our players lost 3-0. In the return match (a month or two later), they won. The team started to develop a game plan that they knew was capable of winning. They also knew that they had developed the skills to execute the game plan. The bank of evidence grew week on week as they started to have more success. By the end of the year, our highest-ranked player faced the world number one in the U.S. Open final ... and beat her.

Here's an important mental note. Many people feel more confident when they have a game plan they believe in and when they know they have the skills to execute it (Australian Institute of Sport, 2010). It makes sense when we consider that 'preparedness' is one of the pillars of confidence (Orlick, 2000).

I was asked to work with a team of senior sales managers in a global financial services corporation a few years ago. My remit was to 'inject belief' into the sales team through the senior managers. During our first workshop together, I asked them to describe their strategy very simply. This was something they really struggled to do. Fundamentally, it seems that their strategy had become overcomplicated. Over the years it had evolved and been amended so many times that it became unwieldy. Nobody really understood it. Therefore, they didn't have a great deal of faith in it. Step One in our task was to produce a strategy (game plan) that everyone had confidence in. The senior management team worked to produce a simple but effective strategy that they had complete belief in, and which they knew they had the ability to deliver. Once we had that, the 'belief' was relatively easy.

How confident would you be if you knew you had a solid game plan and you knew that you had the skills to execute it? How would you feel if you had tried and tested it in challenging situations and it had given you success? What if it had been successful against tougher challenges than the one you were about to face? I'd guess that you'd *know* you could perform well.

There are some fundamental guidelines that will help to grow confidence.

- Have a great game plan.
- Know the processes you need to deliver.
- Focus on the processes.
- Evaluate the processes.
- Become confident that you can deliver the processes.
- Know that when you deliver the process, the performance will follow and your chances of achieving the results are much higher.

"The question that we ask tends to dictate the answer".

Anon

If we ask, "How confident are you that you will win?" we will get a different answer than if we asked, "How confident are you that you will perform well?" It's important that we remember our job. What is your 'two lengths of the pool'? We need to get the job right because it will have a knock-on effect to our confidence. If we think our job is to beat the world record holder or win the gold medal, we might not feel particularly confident we can do it. However, if the job is simply to swim two lengths of the pool as fast as we can, the chances are we'll be more confident in our ability to do it. In fact, that example is absolutely true to life. In 2006, Chris (whose job was actually to swim two lengths of the pool as quick as he could) competed in the Commonwealth Games in Melbourne. We had been so focused on his 'two lengths' mantra that it stayed with him in competition. When he took to the blocks for the Commonwealth final, he was lined up against seven other competitors. On paper, he was not the fastest swimmer in the race. However, he'd qualified pretty strongly and was swimming well. He has a specific game plan, which he knew and trusted. The game plan was built on hitting a specific stroke rate for the first length, so that he could finish the race strongly. He had practiced the race plan and knew he could execute it. For the last few years, he'd been completely dedicated to getting his two lengths absolutely right. This focus was so strong that he took it into the race. In the Commonwealth final his job was still to swim two lengths of the pool as fast as he could. The job didn't change just because he happened to be in a major final.

The starter fired the pistol, and the swimmers took to the water. Chris managed to execute his first length as per his race plan and turned in 5th place at the halfway mark. Because he managed to deliver the first length as planned, he turned at the wall and knew that he could finish strongly. In the second length he powered through the field and won the race. His job was not to win the gold medal. His job was to swim two lengths of the pool as quickly as he could. Chris did his job. He managed to swim his two lengths quicker than everyone else and therefore won the gold. After the race he was interviewed by Sharron Davies, from the BBC. She asked him how it felt to have won the gold.

His answer … "I don't know. I was just swimming two lengths of the pool as quick as I could".

If that strategy is good enough to win a gold medal, it could well work for you. It applies equally to managing a business, to sales, to education, to medicine or any other walk of life you care to think of. Gary Dayton (2007) applies the same principles to trading stocks and shares. If we use very basic strategies to control our own confidence, we are likely to perform well in what we do. When we perform well, we are likely to enjoy ourselves. If we're performing well and enjoying ourselves, we're likely to be motivated to keep doing it.

In summary ...

- Evaluate honestly and objectively.
- Build on what you *can* do.
- Know that you have a great game plan and the knowledge, skill, resources and desire to execute it.
- Remember the simple job and stick to the processes.

References

Australian Institute of Sport (2010) *Self Confidence: Athlete Tipsheet*, Canberra: Australian Institute of Sport.

Bandura, A. (1997) *Self-Efficacy: The Exercise of Control*, New York: Worth Publishers.

Branden, N. (1984) *Honoring the Self*, London: Bantam Press.

Branden, N. (2001) *The Psychology of Self-Esteem: A Revolutionary Approach to Self-Understanding that Launched a New Era in Modern Psychology*, New York: Jossey-Bass.

Clash, M.J. (2003) *Forbes to the Limits: Pushing Yourself to the Edge in Adventure and in Business*, New York: Wiley.

Dayton, G. (2007) 'Trading psychology – The universal law of trading confidence', *Trading Psychology Edge*, September 2007.

Hayes, K., Maynard, I., Thomas, O. and Bawden, M. (2007) 'Sources of confidence identified by world class sport performers', *Journal of Applied Sport Psychology*, 19(4), 434–456.

Horn, T. (2008) *Advances in Sport Psychology*, Champaign, IL: Human Kinetics.

McDonald, J., Orlick, T. and Letts, M. (1995) 'Mental readiness in surgeons and its links to performance excellence in surgery', *Journal of Pediatric Orthopedics*, 15(5), 691–697.

Orlick, T. (2000) *In Pursuit of Excellence: How to Win in Sport and Life Through Mental Training (3rd Edition)*, Champaign, IL: Human Kinetics.

Master Motivation   5

Every sports team and athlete I've ever worked with wants to win. But some want it more than others.

I've been known to start sessions with junior international squads by saying, "Hands up if you want to be a world champion or a world record holder". As you might imagine, all the hands go up. And then I say something that shocks them.

"I don't believe you.

Want to know why?

It's because I've just watched you training".

Then, I go on to explain ..

"When the coach told you to give it 100 percent ... you gave it 80 percent".

"When the coach was giving instructions ... you were talking to your mate".

"When the coach told you to swim hard all the way to the wall ... you cruised in for the last five meters".

"That's not what world champions do!"

Of course, it sounds obvious to say that success in life requires us to be highly motivated. But what exactly does that mean? The members of the junior international squad were motivated, but perhaps not motivated enough to become world champions.

In my experience, world class performers do those things their competitors don't do ... or more specifically ... won't do.

In psychology, motivation is often known as the 'why of behavior'. It helps to explain why we do the things we do and even why we don't do the things

DOI: 10.4324/9781003181491-6

we should do. There are reasons behind our decisions and our actions, which all stems from our motivation (Rabideau, 2005).

Why does a swimmer get out of bed at 4 a.m. on a cold, wet Tuesday in December, drive all the way to the pool and swim up and down for two hours? Why do they then have a bite of breakfast before doing a strength and conditioning session, followed by an hour of physiotherapy, a bite of lunch, a meeting with the performance analyst, a meeting with the coach and back in the pool for another two hours? What's it all in aid of? Why do they do all this, six or seven days a week, for years on end?

The foundation of motivation is *the reason*. We need a reason to do something, or a reason not to. Often, we forget the importance of this. We slip into doing things out of habit. We go through the motions. We lose motivation because we lose sight of the reason.

Sometimes our *reason* morphs, without our realizing it. Sportsmen and women fall into this trap frequently. They often start playing sport because it is fun, and they simply love doing it. For many, they then start to become successful, and their reason starts to change (Deci, Ryan & Koestner, 1999; Jowett & Lavallee, 2007). The sport then becomes a vehicle to achieve success and recognition. Their reason starts to evolve and becomes oriented around winning. A lot of coaches might see this as a good thing. Shouldn't athletes be motivated and driven to win? Isn't that the point? Surely the athletes that are motivated by winning are the ones who are most likely to be successful. They have a hunger and a desire for success that drives them.

In reality, it can be a double-edged sword. What if the athlete is not experiencing success? What if they are not winning? If their reason for participating is to win, the reason could well disappear. If that happens, motivation will evaporate very quickly. I've known many athletes to quit their sport because they hit a tough patch. Their motivation wasn't robust and couldn't carry them through. The irony is that they will say they quit because they weren't enjoying it anymore.

Several psychological experiments have shown how motivation can change very quickly (Deci et al., 1999). When children engage in fun tasks, such as drawing, they will often do it simply because they enjoy it. If those children are then given rewards for doing these tasks, they will often choose not to do them if the rewards are taken away. Their motivation changes from engaging in the task simply because they enjoy it, to only engaging in order to receive a reward. In psychological terms, the motivation shifts from being intrinsic (generated from within), to being extrinsic (generated by some external influence). This is the same pattern that is often seen in athletes who shift from participating because they love the sport, to participating in order to win and receive recognition (Deci & Ryan, 1985).

Of course, there are always a variety of motives that can influence a person (Elliot & Dweck, 2005). It is rare that there is one motive alone. In reality there are probably a number of reasons. However, there will be one or two that are dominant. The same is true within an organization.

Why do people engage in their work?

If we talked to everyone in an office, we'd find a range of motives for each person, and therefore a wide variety of motives present within the organization. Is it for social reasons or because people love being part of a good team? Do they genuinely love the task? Are they motivated by the satisfaction of achieving or winning? Perhaps their motivation is driven by meeting the expectations of their peers or their managers?

The fact is, there are a host of different reasons why people engage in their work (Linder, 1998). In order to understand motivation, we need to start understanding the reasons. This is something that some organizations have already started. The Times 100 (2010) case study shows that the manufacturing giant Siemens has embraced this idea. They realize that their staff are motivated by the challenge of problem solving, the freedom to be creative, to use their imagination and the opportunity to experience a variety of stimuli. In fact, Siemens's motivational strategy recognizes that many people are motivated by the prospect of achieving their potential; what Abraham Maslow would call 'self-actualization' (Maslow, 1970, 1998).

Over the years, I have asked the question, "What's your 'why'?" hundreds of times. Often, I ask people why they do the job that they do, or work for the organization they're in. Interestingly, I've noticed that the answers have all fallen into four categories. I describe it by saying, "Motivation is P.E.A.R. shaped".

P.E.A.R. is, of course, an acronym.

P stands for 'Purpose'

Some people are motivated because they understand the intrinsic value of what they do. They know that they are making a difference and having a positive impact. In many cases they know that they are contributing to something that has genuine importance. Many people are motivated by the knowledge that what they do changes lives for the better or has a positive impact on the world.

E stands for 'Enjoyment'

Many people are motivated because they enjoy what they do. This enjoyment can come because the task is fun. Often it comes because they feel like they're good at it. On many occasions, people enjoy the challenge and the stimulation that comes when we're pushing ourselves. Others may enjoy working with a great team, or great customers. There are a variety of ways to experience enjoyment.

A stands for 'Achievement' (and also ambition)

It won't surprise you to know that this motivates many athletes. Many athletes work for years to win a gold medal. But, as a friend of mine once said, "The medal is just a metal disc on a ribbon". To understand what's really motivating these athletes, we need to know what winning the medal means. Perhaps it's because the gold medal means they are 'the best'. For others, the real motivation is to achieve their potential or know that they're improving and developing. Either way, they are motivated by 'achievement'.

R stands for 'Reward' (and recognition)

This can come in the form of money, but it's not the only form of reward. For many people, what they do becomes rewarding when they get recognition. This might be formal, for example receiving an award. Equally, it might come in the form of positive feedback and a recognition that they've done a great job.

In my experience, we are all motivated by all of these, but in different proportions. Some people are heavily driven by rewards. Others are primarily purpose-driven. It helps to know what is driving us, because it allows us to start mastering our own motivation. Experience also tells me that if we're overreliant on one of these, we could find that our motivation is vulnerable. For example, if we're highly driven by rewards and making money, we will really struggle if the cash dries up.

I often see these four categories as 'pillars' of motivation. From my perspective, it makes sense to have four strong pillars! If our motivation is too 'one dimensional' (i.e., too dependent on one pillar), it tends to be unstable and vulnerable.

This all goes to show that motivation is a pretty diverse concept. It's not simply a case of waving cash in front of an individual to get more effort from them. It helps us realize that people's motivation is very rarely 'all or nothing' and that it is something we can develop.

It's easy to let circumstances dictate our motivation. Athletes often find it's easier to focus their mind if there is a big tournament on the horizon. Athletes also tend to be motivated when they are doing well and winning.

But, what if there's no immediate goal?

What if they're not winning?

If their motivation starts to wane, they can find themselves in a downward spiral. It starts when they begin to take their foot off the gas. They start choosing to do the easier things rather than the difficult things. They don't do quite as many reps in the gym or put quite as much effort into their speed sessions. They get despondent quicker. Rather than sticking with a practice until they make it work, they might try a few times and then give up saying, "It's just not working". If there is a question whether they do a session or postpone, they start choosing to postpone. The end result is a negative downward spiral of reducing performance, reducing confidence and reducing motivation (Elliot & Dweck, 2005).

If we stop paying attention to our processes, the performance will inevitably drop off. If the performance drops off, the results will follow.

The same is true outside of sport. People tend not to approach things as readily if they are not getting the results. Sales executives start to make less sales calls or stop approaching customers. If managers are having difficulties in certain departments, they may delegate that responsibility rather than tackling it head on. It's the same reaction that many of us have to those jobs that always end up at the bottom of the 'to do list' and get put off until tomorrow. The jobs we put off are rarely the ones we understand and are confident in. More commonly, they are the ones we're not sure about. We might not have done them before, or we might have struggled with them in the past. These patterns of deteriorating performance, reflect patterns in the negative performance spirals that we discussed in the opening chapters (Lindsley, Brass & Thomas, 1995).

So, what's the solution? How do we motivate ourselves consistently, throughout all of the ups and down? And how can we motivate others who are struggling?

In order to have strong motivation, we need a reason that is strong, robust and compelling. It has to come from within (Deci & Ryan, 2002). It really is very simple; you have to really want it. You can't make yourself want something because someone else wants you to have it. You will never be truly motivated by the need to please other people. Your motivation has to be genuine and has to come from within. It is not a coincidence that many truly great people have been inspired by their dreams. When they are interviewed, they often talk about the fact that they've been following their dreams (Torres & Weil, 2009). While it sounds obvious, many of us don't follow our dreams. We might think our dreams are silly. We might not believe they are possible. Our dreams might not fit in with everyone else's expectations or plans for us. We might compromise our dreams for other people.

A friend of mine, who was an aspiring entrepreneur, once said to me, "I don't think I have a dream". This intrigued me so I started discussing it with him a little more. When we got a little deeper, it became apparent that he had many dreams and ambitions, but he'd never given them any real recognition. He'd never seen them as *a dream* because they seemed unrealistic. They were not easily achievable, so he'd assigned them to the junk pile. He hadn't honored them, recognized them and nurtured them. He'd never given them any energy or worked on them. Instead, he'd ignored them because he felt they were daft. Ironically, the things he spent his time pursuing were unrelated to his dreams. They were much more realistic, but he wasn't genuinely passionate about them. They were a means to an end.

His motivation was entirely tied to the outcome. Consequently, he flitted from one thing to another and never spent very long on any one project. His motivation petered out when he failed to realize the success he was looking for after a few months. If the project didn't make money quickly, there wasn't any point in it. He was not engaged in the project for its own sake or because he believed in it.

I believe that everybody dreams. The difference between those who follow their dreams, and those who don't, comes down to whether the dreams are honored, recognized and nurtured. Without recognition and energy, our dream will wither. If we give it recognition and energy, it will become strong and vibrant (Seligman, 2005).

The simple truth is this; if we don't honor our dreams, we will never realize them. When we do honor them, believe in them, and believe in ourselves, motivation will always be there. Strong motivation will carry us over the hurdles and help us pick ourselves up when we're stuck in a hole. If you have a dream, a compelling reason to do something, your chances of success skyrocket! If you are doing something purely for an external reason, your motivation will only last as long as the reason remains.

Now that all sounds very idealistic doesn't it. How many people are in a job where they are following their dreams (Linder, 1998)? How many administrators, sales executives or accounts clerks are following their dreams through their careers? Most children aged six or seven years old don't say that they want to be an administrator when they grow up. I'd imagine a stereotypical group of boys would mention the words 'astronaut' or 'footballer' more often than 'recruitment consultant'. So, how can motivation be mastered in situations where we are not absolutely following our heartfelt dreams?

The answer is that we still need a strong and compelling reason (Deci & Ryan, 2002). The activity that we're doing has to mean something to us. It has to be important to us. What benefit is there in doing this job well? What difference would it make if I did it badly? If it's not important to me, there is no reason to do it well (Shah & Gardner, 2008). Why would I invest the time and effort into doing something well, if I could invest half as much and just about scrape through?

A few years ago, I worked for an English Premier League football club. At the time, I saw it as the pinnacle of my career. Many people would probably agree. However, I soon became disillusioned. I had expected that the players would be highly motivated to be the best they could be and to achieve as much as possible for the club. I'll be honest, that was a little naive, I admit. I moved into the football club directly from working in Premiership rugby union. The difference in the motivation of the players was vast. For a while it surprised me. However, the reasons soon became apparent. The footballers were paid many thousands of pounds every week. It actually didn't make any significant material difference to them whether they won or lost. The win bonus was tiny in proportion to their basic salary.

One morning before a game, I chatted to one of our coaches, who'd played the game years before. His basic wage as a player was around £200 per week. The win bonus was also £200 per week. In those days £200 per week bought you a comfortable life with no frills. However, £400 per week bought you a slightly nicer car, a holiday and meals out. Winning made a big difference and consequently the players worked hard. It was similar in the rugby club. Those players who made the England squad had a significantly better lifestyle than those who were squad players in the club. Many of them genuinely aspired to be selected to the international squad because it would make a huge difference to them, both professionally and financially.

There was another fundamental difference between the rugby players and the footballers. In rugby, if you don't work hard in training, you could get hurt on the field. In football, it's unlikely that you'll get hurt. You might lose, but that's about the worst that will happen. As a result, the rugby players were motivated to work.

In reality, our motivation is not normally purely intrinsic or extrinsic. There is often a combination of motives (Deci & Ryan, 1985). Many of our motives may not be intrinsic initially, but our motivation will become stronger if we can start to create a shift towards intrinsic motives. The fact is, our motivation is usually stronger when we can see a gap between the benefits of doing something, and the consequences of not doing it. If we perceive that the gap is large, we tend to be more motivated. If we perceive it to be small, we tend to be less motivated.

Let's take an everyday example. A few chapters ago I mentioned working in a café restaurant business. Our aim was to produce world class cuisine, with world class service. World class for us meant being the best in our sector.

We were not a Michelin-starred restaurant. We were in the leisure dining sector, with the likes of Pizza Express and Frankie & Benny's. Therefore, world class service didn't mean silver service. Our food wasn't gourmet, but it did have to be the best in our sector. Our challenge was to achieve this standard with our team.

Like many businesses, we were pretty picky in our selection process. We spent a great deal of time ensuring we recruited good people. The fact that we had a pretty intense selection process helped our staff understand that we were serious about providing a world class product. In our business, most of the team were either kitchen staff or service staff. In order to ensure that they delivered the greatest possible output, we created an environment that would motivate them to be the best they could be. First, we ensured that our basic rate of pay was slightly higher than our competition. As a result, staff wanted to work for us. We also put a multidimensional incentive package in place, which allowed the staff to benefit when they produced a high standard. We ensured that our incentives ranged from recognition through to rewards. Sometimes, a simple 'well done' or a pat on the back is incredibly motivating for someone. However, we also knew that prizes and cash bonuses did motivate the team. We created a range of incentives that allowed us to give very immediate rewards (on a daily basis) as well as rewards for monthly, quarterly and annual performance. Finally, we structured our incentive program to reward the individuals, the teams (i.e., shift teams) and the staff as a whole when they achieved their targets.

Using the P.E.A.R. shaped motivation approach, this helps create the 'R'.

But, what about the other drivers?

We also worked hard to help people have a sense of purpose in what we were doing. We were a café restaurant business. We served food and drink. Nobody was saving lives. However, they understood that our role was to look after people and create a great experience for them. The team had a little mantra: all of our customers are someone's mum, dad, partner, sister, brother and best friend. So, we look after everyone the way we'd look after our own friends and family. It was something that mattered to them, and they cared about.

We knew that many elements of the work weren't necessarily fun. Very few people would describe cleaning tables or cleaning the toilets as 'fun'. However, we worked to ensure we had a great team, and the environment was enjoyable. And we made sure that everyone had a way to improve and recognize their progress.

We'd created an environment where people knew that what we did was important, and it mattered (P). We had a great team, and an enjoyable place to be (E). They knew that they were really good at their jobs and we, as a business, were at the top of our game (A). And, when we delivered top performance, we got recognized and rewarded (R).

When we built these four pillars within the business, we created something that was incredibly motivating.

We'd created a place where people were proud to belong.

I know this is all pretty small scale. We are not talking about winning Olympic medals or giving mega bonuses, but it shows that by understanding some basic principles and managing the motivational environment, it is possible achieve fantastic performances from a team. The absolute foundation of motivation, as we've already discovered, is *the reason*.

Why would people choose to push themselves?

Why would they work harder?

Why are they going to step outside of their comfort zone?

There has to be a compelling reason!

Managers and coaches can sometimes assume that their team knows *the reason*. At times we can take it for granted that we're all on the same page when, in reality, we may not be. I have made that mistake myself. When working in Premier League football, I was often frustrated when players didn't apply themselves fully to some of the work we were doing. When I reflected on it, there was a possibility that the players didn't really understand why that particular session was important. I assumed that it was perfectly obvious, when in fact it may not have been obvious to the players. As a result, I started to change my approach slightly when I began working for a Championship club in the following season. At the start of every session, I would take one minute to explain the session to the players and the reason we were doing it (I called it my 'Magic One Minute'). I made a point of letting the players know why the session was important and how it contributed to their performance on the field. Unsurprisingly, that one minute proved to be incredibly valuable, and the quality and effort from the players increased dramatically.

It's a simple reminder that they key to motivation is a powerful "Why".

In summary ...

- Know the reason.
- Know why you're doing the task and the importance of doing it well.
- If your reasons have an intrinsic value, they are more likely to be robust and enduring.
- Have a clear focus. A performance profile can be a great tool to do this.
- Honor your dreams!

References

Deci, E.L. and Ryan, R.M. (1985) *Intrinsic Motivation and Self-Determination in Human Behavior*, New York: Plenum.

Deci, E.L. and Ryan, R.M. (2002) *Handbook of Self-Determination Research*, Rochester: University of Rochester Press.

Deci, E.L., Ryan, R.M. and Koestner, R. (1999) 'A meta-analytic review of experiments examining the effects of extrinsic rewards on intrinsic motivation', *Psychological Bulletin*, 125(6), 627–668.

Elliot, A. and Dweck, C.S. (2005) *Handbook of Competence and Motivation*, New York: Guilford Press.

Jowett, S. and Lavallee, D. (2007) *Social Psychology in Sport*, Champaign, IL: Human Kinetics.

Linder, J.R. (1998) 'Understanding employee motivation', *Journal of Extension*, 36(3), 1–8.

Lindsley, D.H., Brass, D.J. and Thomas, J.B. (1995) 'Efficacy-performance spirals: A multi-level perspective', *Academy of Management Review*, 20(3), 645–678.

Maslow, A. (1970) *Motivation and Personality (3rd Edition)*, New York: Harper Row.

Maslow, A. (1998) *Towards a Psychology of Being (3rd Edition)*, New York: Wiley.

Rabideau, S.T. (2005) 'Effects of achievement motivation on behaviour', *Personality Research*, November 2005.

Seligman, M.E.P. (2005) *Authentic Happiness: Using the New Positive Psychology to Realize Your Potential for Lasting Fulfillment*, New York: Free Press.

Shah, J.Y. and Gardner, W.L. (2008) *Handbook of Motivation Science*, New York: Guilford Press.

The Times 100 (2010) 'Siemens: Motivation within a creative environment', *The Times 100 Business Case Studies*. Online. Available www.thetimes100.co.uk/downloads/siemens/siemens_15_full.pdf (accessed 15th December 2010).

Torres, D. and Weil, E. (2009) *Age is Just a Number: Achieve Your Dreams at Any Age in Your Life*, New York: Crown Archetypes.

Deconstructing Pressure   **6**

There is no such thing as pressure.

That might look like a sensationalist statement designed to catch your attention, but actually when you read on you find out it's not quite what it seems. I assure you that the statement is very straightforward and absolutely true. It is one of the great secrets in sport psychology that even the professionals often get wrong. Most sport psychologists and coaches talk about 'managing pressure', which makes the mistake of assuming that it exists.

To be more precise, it's probably more accurate to say that we can only experience pressure in one way – through our imagination. We can only imagine pressure. It's a product of our imagination. Therefore, it's not real.

> "Pressure is nothing more than the shadow of great opportunity".
>
> Michael Johnson

Let's start with the basics. People create pressure for themselves (Beilock, 2010). If we experience 'pressure' it is because we are projecting an imaginary view of the future (Markman, Klein & Suhr, 2008). We use our imagination when we create images and pictures, narratives, fantasies, thought flows and so on (Markman, et al., 2008). Often, we start imagining what might happen if we don't achieve the outcome we desire.

'What if I don't win?'
'What will the press say?'
'What will the coach say?'
'What will people think?'

DOI: 10.4324/9781003181491-7

"Pressure is a word that is misused in our vocabulary. When you start thinking of pressure, it's because you've started to think of failure".

Tommy Lasorda, LA Dodgers Coach

Our imagination is incredibly powerful. Used positively it can help us to optimize our performance. However, we have to be aware that we also use our imagination to create trapdoors for ourselves. To say that pressure is imaginary doesn't mean we can't feel it. It can appear as real as the most vivid dream. But, ultimately, it's still imaginary.

Even if we think other people are putting pressure on us, the truth is that we are the only ones capable of creating pressure (Najemy, 2002). Often people experience pressure if they perceive that they need to meet certain expectations or perceive that a bad performance may meet with negative evaluation from other people (Dunn, 1999; Dunn & Syrotuik, 2003). This phenomenon has also been seen outside of sport, in fields such as performing arts (Sutcliffe, 1997; Harlow, 1999). It is probably something you've experienced yourself at some point in your life. However, expectations, or negative evaluations, don't automatically lead to 'pressure'.

If other people have an expectation of us, it is our choice whether we accept that expectation or not (Glasser, 1999; Valle & Halling, 1989). If I said to you that I expected you to become the world number one tennis player in the next 12 months, you would probably ignore my expectation. You'd think it was completely mad and you'd bin my expectation. You'd choose not to accept it. You can do exactly the same if a manager, coach, teammate, parent, partner or anyone else, tells you they have an expectation of you. However, we often accept expectations from those close to us without questioning them. This is especially true if the person's expectation matches one that we have for ourselves. If your manager tells you that they expect you to hit a certain target, and you agree with them, it's likely that you'd adopt that expectation and use it as a target for yourself.

Like pressure, expectations are also figments of our imagination. They are imaginary projections into the future. Any view of the future must be produced in our imagination, there is nowhere else it can come from (Markman et al., 2008). Expectations could either be a product of your imagination or someone else's. The point is, expectations are not real. They are conjured up in our imagination and in the imagination of other people. It's unwise to let our imagination dictate our thoughts and feelings. However, it is even less wise to let someone else take control of them.

Do you really want your thoughts and emotions to be dictated by someone else's imaginary projections? That's a bit like giving them a remote control for your thoughts and feelings.

It doesn't matter what anyone else expects. Their expectation is irrelevant *because* it comes from their imagination. I'm not trying to be cruel. I'd argue that we are better concerning ourselves with reality, not fantasy. Fantasy is a product of our imagination, just as expectations and pressure are (Markman, et al., 2008). Often people have hopes for us, which they express. We sometimes take those on board as expectations, which we then try to fulfill. If we buy into expectations, we are trying to live up to a fantasy. The best thing to do is to recognize it for what it is and to get on with reality.

Here is an excerpt from a session with an elite junior racket sport player.

> We chatted about how we can construct and deconstruct pressure. As we said, if we experience pressure, it is because we create it. We are the only ones that can ever put pressure on ourselves. We talked about how this worked. When you are thinking about the British Championships, you could create pressure for yourself by thinking … 'I'm number one', 'I'm meant to win', 'what if I don't?', 'what will people think?', 'I expect myself to win', 'I want to win', 'I want my name in lights', etc.
>
> If you think this way, you create this imaginary, illusionary pressure on yourself. However, it doesn't have to be that way. You could choose to deconstruct it. During the session you did a really good job of explaining to me why there was no pressure, namely because you can't change or control anyone else's expectations. If you don't win, then you don't win. If you give it your best, you've done all you can do. It is fine to want to win but it is pointless expecting it.
>
> It is important to remember the job that you have to do. You do not have to win (that's not the job) or be number one (that's not it either). Your only job is to play the best you can on the day – that's it – nothing else!
>
> Remember, you choose the expectations that you accept. If I expect you to become senior England captain next week you choose to ignore that expectation. You can do the same when someone says, 'you should beat her'. So what if they think that. It's completely irrelevant.

Athletes feel 'pressure' when they get *the job* wrong (Lane, 2001). Typically, athletes think that their job is to win, to climb up the rankings, to secure prize money or sponsorship. Sales executives think that *the job* is to hit their sales target. However, none of those things are *the job*. Normally when we get the job wrong, it is because we're too busy focusing on the outcome. Our job is to deliver the process. That is the bit we can control. Our job is not to achieve an outcome. At this point I can see some thought bubbles appearing.

Do I really mean that the job is not to achieve an outcome? Surely that is a cop-out. Aren't we all in the results business? Most of the football managers, head coaches and performance directors I've known would certainly say they were in the results business. That also goes for sales directors, managing directors, chief executives, school principals and just about anyone else. Of course, there is always an outcome that we're working towards, but our focus should not be tied to it. If we focus on the result, we will often forget the process. Many people focus on the result, rather than delivering the processes that would give them the best chance of achieving it. So many people put energy into worrying about what will happen if they don't hit the target, they forget to focus on doing what they need to do (Rotella, 2004).

"We spend so much time worrying about the things we can't control, and too little focusing on the things we can control" (Simon Hartley).

By aiming for the result, we set ourselves a job which is outside of our control (Bull, 1996). The fact that it is outside of our control means that it's uncertain. Winning is never certain. Hitting a target is never certain. There is always an element of uncertainty. This uncertainty is what tends to cause us the angst (Boelen & Reijntjes, 2009). How can we be completely confident in our ability to achieve something that has uncertainty? If you're trying to do an 'impossible' job or even a job which you have no control over, you will probably imagine pressure because you will not be 100 percent sure that you can do the job. The job might seem too big. If the job is to win the tournament, an athlete might doubt their ability to do that. Even a confident athlete won't *know* that they can do that job. There is often a gap between what we believe we can achieve, and what we think we must achieve. That gap manifests as the worry and anxiety we associate with pressure. If we create an expectation for ourselves, we post a target. If we are not absolutely sure that we can achieve that target, we might start to have doubts and worries. If we also give that target some meaning, we will magnify our doubts and worries.

Here is a piece from a report that I wrote for an elite junior golfer after our first session together. The golfer was exceptionally talented but produced 'Jekyll and Hyde' performances – as he described them. He would play extremely well when there was 'no pressure' and was a wreck when 'under pressure'.

> We kicked off by talking about the difference between your round on Saturday (an impressive score) and your round on Sunday (which you weren't happy with). The round on Saturday was a 'nothing event' (as you described it), whereas Sunday's was 'an important' one. You described Saturday's experience by saying that it was like watching

yourself from your living room. The shots seemed to almost play themselves. You likened it to playing a shot where someone pressed the 'save' button. After that it's as if someone pressed 'play' and the shots just kept coming out almost automatically and near-perfectly. You weren't thinking about your shots, you were just playing naturally and enjoying yourself. On Sunday (just 24 hours later) your performance nose-dived. You said you were anxious and felt under pressure. You didn't start particularly well but once you'd made a couple of slight errors, these compounded and the errors started to get bigger and more frequent. You said your game 'fell apart'.

We talked about the difference between the two events. You said that Saturday's game was on your home course. You knew the other competitors and you knew you could beat them. You also said that there was no pressure because it wasn't an important competition. On Sunday there was a trophy at the end of the competition, and you perceived it as being more important. You were playing on a course you'd only played a handful of times and you didn't know who you were competing against. In reality, there is no real difference between the two matches. Your job is the same for each match. You simply have to play the best game of golf you can. You know what you need to do to play good shots. It doesn't matter where you play. Your challenge is simply to play the best shot you can when you get to the ball. It doesn't matter what name they put on the trophy. It doesn't matter whether you're playing against the world number one … or me. Your job is not to beat the opponent, it's to get the ball in the hole in the fewest shots possible. That means simply playing good shots consistently.

We spent a while discussing the reason that winning has been so important to you. This led us on to talking about your dreams of being a really successful PGA Tour Pro. When we discussed this in more depth, you also started talking about wanting the other people to notice how good you are. We chatted about wanting to be successful and almost escape the prospect of a mediocre life, working for 30 years in a factory. You know that you're talented, and I also know you get frustrated when you don't show the world how talented you are. I sense that if you didn't, you'd kick yourself because you'd feel like you'd not made the most of your talent.

There are lots of potential trapdoors here. Wanting to become a successful Tour Pro is fine but, at the moment it is turning a simple shot into a life and death event. If you're not careful, the shot becomes a judgment of how good you are and how successful you are. It also becomes an indicator of whether you can achieve your dreams and escape the prospect of leading an average life. It tells you whether you're doomed to work in the same factory for 30 years or if you can live your dreams. Your imagination starts to create a lot of baggage around the shot, which your mind then turns into pressure. As you now know, pressure doesn't actually exist.

We talked about the danger that golf becomes like a really narrow pinnacle. If you believe that your life depends on being successful in golf, shots start to become a bit like facing a firing squad. If failing at golf means failing as a person, there is a lot to lose if you screw a shot up. You said that losing £15,000 would be a lot of money to you. We talked about the 'pressure' you might feel if you were faced with a three-foot putt that would potentially win or lose you £15,000. If £15,000 was a lot to lose by missing a three-foot putt, compare that to the prospect of losing your hopes and dreams. That is why being successful in life cannot hinge on your performance on the golf course. The trick is to be happy with your life right now. If you know that you can be a success whether you sink the putt or miss it, you're more likely to see it as a simple shot and not a life and death situation.

We talked about the difference between a three-foot putt played on your home course when you are out practising by yourself, and a three-foot putt at Augusta in a competition with a title, prize money and a television audience of millions. The obvious point is that there is no difference .. unless your mind makes it different.

This principle applies not only to golf shots and putting. It is equally true for a sale, or a deal, or an interview, or an exam, or anything else we feel has pressure. It is very rare that we are actually in a life-and-death situation, although sometimes we give situations that meaning (Frankl, 1959/1984). If you have ever watched talent shows on TV (e.g., *The X Factor*), you will see contestants who are incredibly nervous before a performance. The reason they are nervous is because they have decided to pin all their hopes and dreams onto singing a song. Some of them perceive that the success of their life depends on a judge saying, 'yes' or 'no'. In their mind, a 'yes' keeps the hope of stardom alive and a 'no' means that their dreams of leading a successful life are over. It would be a different story if they were already happy with their life and saw the prospects that they had beyond singing. If singing, golf or any other task becomes 'all or nothing', we're likely to create a very strong illusion of pressure that could consume us.

To help us ensure sure we get *the job* right, we need to make sure we don't start attaching meanings to our performance. Sometimes this happens because we take on the hopes and expectations of others. International players often feel that they carry 'the hopes of the nation'.

There's a famous example of this.

It's the 17th July 1994 ... The Rose Bowl, Pasadena, California.

The best footballer in the world, Roberto Baggio, has the last penalty kick in the sudden death shootout. If he scores, Italy stays alive. If he misses, Brazil wins the World Cup. He was the best player in the world at the time. And he missed. He didn't just miss by a whisker. He blazed the ball over the bar.

How is it that the world's best player failed to hit the target from 12 yards?

Was he simply focused on taking the shot? Or, was he conscious of the thousands of Italian fans in the stadium? Was he imagining the millions at home in Italy, glued to their television sets? Did he feel like he was carrying the hopes and dreams of the nation?

Normally the issue becomes further exacerbated when our ego becomes involved (Metzinger, 2010). It's possible that some athletes buy into the media hype because they have tied themselves so closely to the media. The media is the vehicle that provides them with a public image and a public profile. Without that public profile and image, footballers (for example) would not be paid hundreds of thousands of pounds every week to kick balls around. If it wasn't for the media's insatiable appetite for football, the players would not be household names. So, there is far more likelihood that the players will care about what the media says and how they are portrayed. Their image and their profile become paramount. All of a sudden, the game is more than just 22 players on a grass pitch with a ball, two goals and a trio of officials. It becomes an exercise in making sure that the media and social media are behind them. The players are likely to focus on the sizable difference between doing well, and the media benefits that brings, compared to doing badly with the negative media coverage with its knock-on effect to the players' lives. If this happens, the chances are that the players will get *the job* wrong. They might start thinking that their job is to impress. They may perceive a 'need to win' so that they can save face and be portrayed well. Perhaps they become focused on the need to become a hero, or avoid becoming a villain, rather than focusing on playing football.

... and so, the illusion of pressure is born in their minds.

When the game becomes more than just the game, we have got the game wrong.

When a tennis match become more than just a game between two players with rackets, a ball and a net and some white lines, we're not playing tennis anymore. If the game becomes a chance to impress someone, or a means of getting recognition, or a way of paying back the parents who have spent a fortune so far, it's not a game of tennis anymore. Instead, we are playing a game we have absolutely no control over. We cannot control whether someone else is impressed with us. We cannot control whether someone gives us recognition. It is not our job to pay our parents back through our performances. If parents choose to support our sport, their choice should be made purely because they love to support us in whatever we do. It should not be dependent on our performances, winning, rankings or titles. None of those things are our job.

As we've said already, we create pressure therefore we can 'deconstruct it' (Manz, 2002). The easiest way is not to create it in the first place. However, if we do feel pressure, we have the ability to dismantle it and start to see the reality rather than the illusion. One of the best ways to do this is to simply find all the reasons why there is no pressure in a situation. If you start to perceive pressure, take a few moments to remind yourself why there is no pressure and never was any pressure. Normally this involves a slight reality check and a quick reminder of the job. Once we do that, we are more likely to be able to focus on exactly what we need to do in that moment. In reality, the job we need to do will normally be pretty simple and something we're very capable of doing. Rather than trying to 'serve for the match' or 'win Championship point', we'll simply be trying to serve. Instead of trying to win the World Cup, the job is simply to take a penalty kick. Rather than attempting to win the Ryder Cup, the job is simply to execute a three-foot putt (Fisher, 1998).

When working with an international squash team, I often heard them referring to 'big points'. Of course, I understood what they were referring to, but I asked them how many points a *big point* was worth. Is it worth three points, or five or ten? Naturally the answer is that the big points are worth one point, the same as all the others. However, because the players perceived them differently, they played them differently. *Match point* is a classic example. Instead of doing the very good things that got them to match point against the world number one, they would change and try something completely different. They would force a shot that wasn't really on. Their patience and composure would desert them, and they'd try to play a winner too early. So often they would end up losing by the odd point because they started to play differently right at the end. They started to perceive pressure in the *big points*. Interestingly, this pattern happened in *big events*, against *big opponents* or in *big points*. Rather than simply playing the ball and playing the point in front of them, they started to inject a different meaning to it all. When they started to accept that every point was equal, and that the competition or the opponent was irrelevant, they were able to play their shots more naturally. When they ditched the mental baggage, they began to play each point on its own merit and play one point at a time.

Once performers have got the hang of deconstructing pressure, I like to start stress-testing it with them to see how robust it is. Like many things, it's easy to ditch pressure in a classroom environment or a training session. It's a greater challenge in the heat of competition. To put it into a practical setting, I often use 'pressure training' exercises (Taylor & Wilson, 2005). In reality, that is probably a daft name. The aim of 'pressure training' is simple. The performer's task is simply to stick to their job, even though we may throw things at them to tempt them away. I work with the coach to create a set of scenarios and challenges which tempt the performer out of sticking to their simple job. Some refer to this as mental toughness (Jones, Hanton & Connaughton, 2007).

Let's look at an example of pressure training with the elite junior golfer who produced the 'Jekyll and Hyde' performances. We started on the putting green. Once we had identified some simple things to focus on, he set about putting. He took some shots from various distances and from different positions on the green, sinking 8/10. I then added a simple challenge. If he scored eight in his next ten shots, his dad would buy him a CD (for the younger generations, 'CD' stands for Compact Disc). If he scored less than six, he had to wash his dad's car. The golfer's challenge was simple. He just had to keep playing the shots as he did before I introduced the challenge. This principle is one that can be applied very easily to a host of different situations. The introduction of competition is a simple challenge, which tempts many to start playing differently. Introducing competition with a reward for winners and a consequence for losers often adds to the challenge. With an international archery squad, the losers were required to clear up, carry the bags and do the chores for the winners. Even simple things like asking players to put £20 into an envelope, which will be the prize for the winner, adds a dimension. However, there are other things that often cause people to forget the simple job. Those who like structure can often get flustered if their routine is broken or their preparation is interrupted. The job is to perform at your best. Sometimes things happen that will disrupt preparations and routines. However, the job is still to do the best you can and focus on delivering the performance. For people who live for positive feedback from others, generating a negative atmosphere can draw them away from doing the simple job. The job was never to please other people or to elicit positive feedback. The job has always been to perform as well as you can. Therefore, providing negative feedback is often a real test. All of the scenarios that we present are designed to test how robustly a performer can stick to the simple job. If negative feedback from their coach affects their performance, it is because they are still trying to impress the coach. If losing has an effect, it is because they still believe the job is to win.

The basis of *pressure training* is the same as any other form of training. In order to get better, we need a challenge that is slightly beyond our current capabilities. It is the same principle that we employ when we're trying to get fit. You can't expect to get fitter by running the same distance at the same speed. We won't increase our ability simply by doing the same things in the same way. At best you'll maintain your level, but you won't increase it. To improve, we need to push our boundaries and step outside of our comfort zone.

In summary ...

- Pressure is a product of our imagination.
- We normally experience pressure when we attach meanings to the performance and focus on the outcome.
- It is exacerbated when our ego gets involved.
- Deconstruct pressure by seeing the job for what it really is.
- Put your mind to the test. Stress-test, to see how robust it is.

References

Beilock, S. (2010) *Choke*, New York: Free Press.

Boelen, P.A. and Reijntjes, A. (2009) 'Intolerance of uncertainty and social anxiety', *Journal of Anxiety Disorders*, 23, 130–135.

Bull, S.J. (1996) *The Mental Game Plan: Getting Psyched for Sport*, London: Sport Dynamics.

Dunn, J.G.H. (1999) 'A theoretical framework for structuring the content of competitive worry in ice hockey', *Journal of Sport & Exercise Psychology*, 21, 259–278.

Dunn, J.G.H. and Syrotuik, D.G. (2003) 'An investigation of multidimensional worry dispositions in high contact sport', *Psychology of Sport & Exercise*, 4, 265–282.

Fisher, M. (1998) *The Golfer and the Millionaire*, New York: Cassell Illustrated.

Frankl, V.E. (1959/1984). *Man's Search for Meaning*, New York: Touchstone.

Glasser, W. (1999) *Choice Theory: A New Psychology of Personal Freedom*, New York: Harper Collins.

Harlow, J. (1999) 'Fear drives actors from the stage', *The Sunday Times*, 14th February. p. 13.

Jones, G., Hanton, S. and Connaughton, D. (2007) 'A framework for mental toughness in the world's best performers', *The Sport Psychologist*, 21, 243–264.

Lane, A. (2001) 'Relationship between perceptions of performance expectations and mood amongst distance runners', *Journal of Science and Medicine in Sport*, 4(1), 116–128.

Manz, C.C. (2002) *The Power of Failure*, San Francisco: Berrett-Koehler.

Markman, K.D., Klein, W.M.P. and Suhr, J.A. (2008) *Handbook of Imagination and Mental Simulation*, London: Psychology Press.

Metzinger, T. (2010) *The Ego Tunnel: The Science of the Mind and the Myth of the Self*, New York: Basic Books.

Najemy, R. (2002) *The Psychology of Happiness*, New York: Holistic Harmony.

Rotella, R.J. (2004) *The Golfer's Mind*, New York: Free Press.

Sutcliffe, P. (1997) 'Out of tune with the rest of us', *The Sunday Times*, 8th June 2007. p. 6. (Supplement: Stress Manager, Part 4: Raising Your Game).

Taylor, J. and Wilson, G.S. (2005) *Applying Sport Psychology: Four Perspectives*, Champaign, IL: Human Kinetics.

Valle, R. and Halling, S. (1989) *Existential-Phenomenological Perspectives in Psychology: Exploring the Breadth of Human Experience*, New York: Plenum Press.

Love Your Discomfort Zone

7

Most of us like to operate in our comfort zone. By definition, our comfort zone encompasses those things that we're familiar with, that we know and are confident in (Bardwick, 1995; White, 2009; Cotterill & Johnson, 2008). In fact, Alistair White (2009) refers to it as a state, in which a person operates in an 'anxiety-neutral condition', using a limited set of skills to deliver steady performance, normally with low risk. Tasks that fall into our comfort zone are those which we are competent at, confident in and find relatively easy. We don't tend to find these sorts of tasks terribly demanding or challenging.

It is possible that we can engage in a task which we'd consider to be well within our comfort zone, but in a situation which lies outside of it. For example, a rugby goal kicker might be taking a regulation kick on a poor surface, with a crosswind and driving rain. The task is not particularly demanding, but the situation pushes the performer into their discomfort zone.

Although our comfort zone is quite a cozy place to be, in many ways it's also a dangerous place to be (Bardwick, 1995). We don't tend to develop or improve when we operate in our comfort zone. We do not tend to learn very much in our comfort zone. Geoff Colvin (2008) notes that to excel in any field, we need to engage in a great deal of *deliberate practice*. In fact, *deliberate practice* is seen by many as the foundation for expertise and exceptional performance (Ericsson & Charness, 1999). Interestingly, Geoff Colvin notes that *deliberate practice* is often uncomfortable, which is why not many people do it and why not many people truly excel in what they do.

Many people believe that we would become more confident by doing tasks we're comfortable and familiar with. However, our confidence becomes limited to those things that are within our comfort zone. Our tendency often is to restrict ourselves to doing those things we are comfortable with, and we start to shy away from things which would push us into uncharted territories.

DOI: 10.4324/9781003181491-8

In a sense, we create a more solid wall around our comfort zone which starts to act as a barrier, stopping us from attempting new challenges. We start to believe that if we can't do something right now, we won't be able to do it and so we don't even attempt it. This is one of the strongest reasons for regularly operating in your discomfort zone and always challenging yourself to push the envelope. The evidence will tell you that you can take on new challenges and become good at things you've never tried before.

We grow when we enter our discomfort zone. By consistently exposing ourselves to challenges and demands, we develop and learn. In fact, our comfort zone gradually expands to include the new challenges. As we become more familiar with the demands and become more competent in them, those situations and tasks become comfortable. Let's look at some simple examples ...

Example 1

In Chapter 4 (Control Your Confidence), we looked at the strategy that we employed with the England Squash team. The program deliberately took them outside of their comfort zone and challenged them in new ways. Pitching them against faster, more powerful, and harder hitting opponents was definitely uncomfortable for them. Before engaging in the program, it was something they avoided doing. However, there was another dimension to the discomfort zone that we created. A few months previously, the team had struggled to perform in a World Team Championship event. They were odds on favorites to win on paper, but they ended up losing the final to the host team in front of their home fans. When I spoke to the players, they started talking about the pressure of the event and how the media and supporters in the U.K. expected them to win. Knowing this, we made sure that the test matches that we set up for the team were all covered in the squash media. We created some media hype around the matches. This all served to create a multidimensional challenge to the players. Gradually their comfort zone grew to encompass the things they were previously uncomfortable with. As a result, the team won the European Team Championship comfortably and our top player beat the 'fast, powerful and hard hitting' world number one the following autumn.

Example 2

I worked for several years in Premiership rugby union. One year I watched one of our players at work. He is a very good professional and works extremely hard on his game. One of the key facets of his game is kicking. I used to watch his kicking sessions with great interest. The player would consistently set himself difficult challenges that were well outside of his comfort zone. He would often aim at a very small target and challenge himself to hit the target repeatedly. For example, he may aim at a single post from 20 meters and challenge himself to hit it ten times in a row. If he hit nine but missed the tenth, he'd go back and start again from zero. Once he'd done ten, he would increase the challenge. He might increase the distance or work against a crosswind to make it harder. It would be the same if he was kicking out of hand. As the practice progressed, he would increase his precision and accuracy, or have players charge at him to reduce his time and space. I started to realize that the player was actively using his discomfort zone to make himself a better player. Whenever a practice became comfortable, he'd change it to make it uncomfortable again. As a result, he became a better player. He was able to produce difficult skills, executed precisely, with very little time or space.

Example 3

I actively encourage people to understand their comfort zone and their discomfort zone, and to seek out opportunities to enter their discomfort zone. A swimmer that I worked with for many years became very adept at doing this. On one occasion he entered a competition in Eastern Europe because he knew it would be challenging and uncomfortable. He knew that getting there would be reasonably difficult because it was off the beaten track. He knew that the accommodation would be far from luxurious, the food would be basic, and the pool would be cold. Importantly, he also knew that the competition would be dominated by young, keen and talented Eastern Europeans who were all competing on their own doorstep. The opposition would all be in race condition (rested, tapered and shaved), because this was one of their big events of the year. In comparison, our swimmer knew that he was in the middle of a heavy training phase and was fatigued. Many athletes would probably have entered the competition with their excuses already lined up. However, his job was to go and perform at his best, even though many of the conditions were against him. One of the aims of the exercise was to deliberately put him in a situation that exposed any cracks in his performance. We needed to see any potential weaknesses so that we could work on them and strengthen them.

He also selected meets in which he would face some of his major opponents in Europe, and the world, head-to-head. Rather than choosing opportunities that would give him the best chance of beating them, he chose times when the odds were against him. On one occasion, he competed in the middle of a very heavy block of training. I remember the athlete telling me that he was stiff and sore as he stood on the blocks ready to start the race. In comparison, his main opponent was race ready. Despite this, he finished a very close second and only slightly outside of his personal best. These experiences also taught him that he could perform in tough situations. He could produce a swim just outside of his personal best when he was tired and sore. He didn't need perfect preparation to swim fast. If his preparation was thrown out for some reason, or he didn't physically feel on top of the world, he knew that he could pull out a good time anyway. That knowledge only came because he deliberately stepped into his discomfort zone. He sought to become comfortable with those things he was unsure about or uncomfortable with.

Of course, there are many parallels outside of sport. Business people and entrepreneurs often do the same. It's also true of surgeons, teachers, musicians, traders (Wolfinger, 2008) and many other walks of life. They take on new challenges, they innovate, they push the envelope. The world of business is incredibly dynamic, as is medicine, education, science, the performing arts, and every other field you care to think of. As a human race, if we didn't step into our discomfort zone, we would never have discovered anything. Explorers would never have charted the earth. Technologists would never have invented the microchip. NASA would never have launched anything into space. On a much more personal level, peak performances occur when we operate on the edge of our capability (Csikszentmihalyi, 1990). These innovations are not a product of the comfort zone, they are a product of the discomfort zone.

I come across a common challenge for executives and managers in business environments. Many of them have similar discomfort zones. They tend to feel comfortable when they feel in control. However, this can become dysfunctional when they are managing other people. The challenge for many is to relinquish control and allow others to take control in certain situations. This requires a great deal of trust. I notice that this is particularly common in business owners or CEOs (Aronoff, 2011). Much of my work with executives revolves around helping them enter this discomfort zone. Initially, they don't see it as part of their discomfort zone because it doesn't involve working harder, working longer or increasing their targets. When we stop and look at it though, the reality becomes obvious. Relinquishing control is clearly in their discomfort zone because they are uncomfortable with the prospect, and they typically find it so hard to do.

So why don't we all habitually launch into our discomfort zones? There are several potential reasons. Some people might see this as risk-taking. Some people initially don't like the sensation of being uncomfortable. When we enter the discomfort zone, we often encounter uncertainty and a loss of control. I know from personal experience that sometimes the discomfort zone can be an almost scary place. I often step a long way into my discomfort zone, sometimes beyond the discomfort zone and into the *pain zone* on the other side. The further out you go, the more out of your depth you feel. There are fewer familiar landmarks. The world you see often seems a lot different to the world you're used to. There is often an incredibly steep learning curve. We often experience a series of setbacks (Heath, 2009). We encounter hurdles that we've never crossed before and questions we have never been asked before. Inevitably it requires a lot more work. We sometimes take emotional hits along the way if we don't get the results we were looking for after all our efforts. We could start to question ourselves and ask whether we're actually capable of taking on the challenge we've set ourselves. It may take a long time to see results. As we noted in Chapter 4 (Control Your Confidence), our confidence will be more fragile if it is based on results. Therefore, to be happy stepping into our discomfort zone, we need to ensure that we evaluate our processes, rather than judge our results (Gallwey, 1986; Dayton, 2007).

We've all had experiences like this. I remember back to those very early days of parenthood when we really didn't know what we were doing at times. Everything was new and unfamiliar. There were so many questions that we didn't have the answers to and situations we'd never encountered before. I also remember setting up businesses and working in new sectors and industries. The experience was very similar in many ways. There were an awful lot of setbacks, and I tripped over a lot of hurdles.

The greatest hurdle for many people is often the risk of failure. This risk may even be a barrier which keeps them locked in their comfort zone. The perception of failure often causes people who enter their discomfort zone to endure it rather than embrace it and love it (Heath, 2009). The title of the chapter is 'Love Your Discomfort Zone'. It is important to *love* it not just to endure it. If we love something, we're much more likely to seek it out. If we endure something, we're likely to only do it if we feel we have to. More often than not, we'll avoid doing it if possible. One of the best illustrations is physical exercise. Some people actively enjoy pushing their bodies. They like the feeling that their muscles are working and that they are out of breath. They like to know that they are testing themselves and pushing their capability. Personally, I like to know that I can do more today than I did last week. However, there are people who couldn't imagine anything worse. They can't understand why people would want to be out of breath, hot, sweaty, and aching. Consequently, they will avoid exercise where possible, and do as little as possible when they absolutely have to exercise.

Fundamentally, we need to be happy making mistakes if we are to love our discomfort zone. We have to accept and embrace the fact that we will not get it right first time. In fact, we have to know that there may be some catastrophic failures along the way (Hartley, 2018). Making mistakes, as we all know, is an essential part of learning. Sometimes our greatest errors can be our most powerful lessons (Heath, 2009; Halden-Brown, 2003). If we are scared of making mistakes, and scared of failing, we will probably stay firmly trapped inside our comfort zone. After all, when we're doing the things we're confident in and familiar with, we stand much more chance of getting them 'right'. When we get things 'right' we get that nice warm fuzzy feeling inside. When we get things 'wrong' our ego takes a knock, which tends not to feel nice. There is also a chance that other people will notice. If that's the case, we also stand a chance of looking daft.

Here is a short piece from an article that I wrote for *Squash Player* magazine, which was entitled 'Learn from everything'.

> 'I've missed more than 9000 shots in my career. I've lost almost 300 games. 26 times, I've been trusted to take the game winning shot and missed. I've failed over and over and over again in my life. And that is why I succeed'.
>
> Michael Jordan is not alone. Most of the great people who have ever lived, have failed. Many of the great entrepreneurs went bust numerous times before they made serious money. The great artists and composers have torn up more work than they ever publish. Great athletes always miss more than they score and make more duff shots than perfect shots. And, as Michael Jordan says, that is the reason they succeed.
>
> It's funny how most people hate making mistakes. As human beings, we tend to view mistakes as negative. We tend to view bad performances as negative and view losing as negative. In reality though, it's not the case. I agree that it's usually uncomfortable at the time because we want things to work perfectly all the time. We want things to come off perfectly first time and often get frustrated if the results don't show quickly enough.
>
> Everyone knows that making mistakes is an important part of the learning process. However, there are relatively few people that embrace mistakes and celebrate them, or even who see them as a positive. Common advice is to forget about bad performances and put them behind you. However, the impact of losing or performing badly does often drive people to work harder on their game. Daft as it sounds, most people learn the least about their performance from victories or successes.
>
> One of the characteristics of a truly great athlete is that they learn from everything – the good, the bad and the average. They learn

from wonderful performances and dire performances equally. Those truly great athletes realize that to stay ahead they don't just need to move forwards. They actually need to move forwards quicker than everyone else, or they'll get overtaken. At the very pinnacle of every sport are athletes who have to constantly improve their game. They have to get better after every single training session and every single match they play. If they don't, they know that someone will overtake them.

Hartley (2010)

Human beings make mistakes. Sport psychologist and equestrian coach, Susan Halden-Brown (2003) suggests that mistakes are not only inevitable, but also incredibly useful in sport. This sentiment is echoed by Tal Ben-Shahar (2009), who would advise us to forget about trying to eliminate mistakes and forget about trying to be perfect in life. Not only is it futile, but it stops us from growing, being happy and living our lives to the full.

Imagine if we scrapped the concept of 'right' and 'wrong' for a moment. I don't mean that we ditch our values and become criminals. I simply mean that we drop the labels and the judgment we apply. If we could stop judging our efforts as 'right' or 'wrong', or as 'good' or 'bad', we can start to see them for what they actually are. Let's also imagine for a moment that it really didn't matter what other people thought. What if we weren't that interested in whether we looked good? What if we didn't care if we looked a bit daft? What if we didn't care whether people talked about us behind our backs or not? Imagine if you felt free to try something, knowing that if it didn't work perfectly, it didn't matter. What if you just could try something knowing that mistakes were fine? In their book, *The Art of Possibility*, Zander and Zander (2000) write about an orchestra rehearsal. During the rehearsal, someone made a mistake. Zander, the conductor, stopped and said, 'How fascinating!' There was no judgment or negative reaction because the mistake was not 'wrong'. Let's take a step further and imagine that mistakes were actually celebrated because they were an essential part of learning, developing, and growing? What if we saw mistakes and failure the same way as Michael Jordon does?

As human beings we have an infinite power to choose how we experience the world. Therefore, we have the choice to decide how we define success and failure (Manz, 2000, 2002). We can choose whether our discomfort zone is a threatening place because within it there is the prospect that we could fail. Our perception of mistakes and failure dictates how we feel. The meanings that we apply to the words 'mistakes' and 'failure' will underpin how we view them. We could embrace mistakes, knowing that they are constructive.

We could redefine our view of failure. Some people would not perceive that they'd failed, simply because they attempted something that didn't work. Instead, they would see failure as not having attempted in the first place (Hartley, 2018).

During the last few years, I have been incredibly privileged to watch my children learn to walk. Just watching them has taught me a huge amount about learning and achievement. The first thing I noticed was that they both fell down a lot. In fact, in the early stages they fell down constantly. In conventional terms, their success to failure ratio registered a 100 percent failure rate. This didn't just continue for a day or two. It continued for several weeks, with many attempts every day. If we adults had tried multiple attempts per day for several weeks with a 100 percent failure rate, we would probably have given up. Of course, infants don't give up, they keep trying. The difference is, they have no concept of failure. To them, falling over isn't 'wrong'. It's not a 'mistake'. So, they kept on trying. They didn't try the same way each time, they changed slightly and adapted. Gradually they started to change the success to failure ratio. They would balance just for a moment, then take a step, then two. They start to use supports less and walk independently more of the time. I'm sure you know the rest of the story.

The critical difference between children learning to walk, and most of us attempting something new is the perception of failure. Infants don't have any concept of failure, so they keep going. Many adults try a handful of times and give up if it's not perfect. How many times have you heard, or uttered, the words, 'I can't do it'. Normally, those words are the *reason* for our 'failure' not the *result* of it. If we changed our perception and said, 'I can't do it perfectly yet', we may try some new ways and eventually succeed.

Criticism is often uncomfortable for us. When I was a student, I remember being disheartened when I took a piece of work to my tutor and found it returned with comments and suggestions (normally written in red ink). I wanted it to come back with just one word on it … 'perfect'. However, that never happened. After a while, my perception started to change. I started using the comments to improve my work and started to think differently about how I approached it. I would try to preempt the comments and make changes before I submitted the work. As I progressed through my studies, I became increasingly frustrated when there were less and less comments. I started to want the suggestions and looked forward to seeing the red ink. The criticism was helping me to get better. I can remember confronting my tutor one day and asking why there was no red ink on my work. Surely the work couldn't be perfect, there had to be something I could do to improve it. I'd started to thrive on the critical comments and knew that they were fueling my growth.

In reality, it is often our ego that prevents us from loving our discomfort zone (Metzinger, 2010). My ego was stung by my tutor's criticism initially. It is our ego that worries about failing or looking silly. The ego worries about what people might think, or how we might be judged. The ego projects the image of what might happen if we get it wrong. And it is our ego that feels the pain if we judge that we have failed at something. I know this from personal experience because I've been there. I've tried things in my businesses that haven't worked out as planned. I've shed tears. I can remember sobbing on the phone to my Mum when we made the decision to move out of our dream house and downsize. The business venture that I'd been working on had not yielded the financial rewards that I needed. I felt like I'd failed. I had attempted something that hadn't worked. We were desperately short of cash, and we had no option other than to move out of the house we loved and into a smaller rental property. That hurt. My ego took a severe hit. My pride was definitely dented. In fact, if my pride had been a car, it would probably have been a write-off.

Transcending our ego is a very important step if we are to love our discomfort zone.

Once we have moved beyond our ego and the fear of making mistakes or failing, we are free to become creative (Robinson, 2010). Creativity is enabled in our discomfort zone. Creativity, by definition, requires us to do something new. It requires innovation. We cannot be truly creative without stepping into the unknown. Creativity requires us to risk failing (Brown, 2008). I recently helped an organization to develop an environment that nurtures creativity. The principles are very simple. First, the environment is free of judgment and allows people to experiment. There is no perfect model and therefore no right way or wrong way to do something. Because there is no right way or wrong way, we are open to new possibilities. We realize that there is a very real chance that somebody could come up with an entirely new solution which no one has ever considered before. The new solution could be far more effective than anything we've seen so far and revolutionize current practice. Human beings are unique. The way we look at the world is unique. Therefore, by allowing everyone the freedom to experiment, we give ourselves the best chance of finding new solutions.

Here is a very practical illustration from *Street Soccer Coaching*, which is a handbook on creative coaching.

> The most effective way of producing a skill for one person will be different for another. Even the way each player kicks a ball will be individual. Every player's body is different; they have different sized feet, their limbs are different lengths, their weight is distributed differently,

their center of gravity is located in a different place in their body, their muscles are different sizes and all have different strength. So, how does it make sense to ask every player to conform to a textbook model?

Added to this, every player has a unique neurological system. The neural networks in our brain and our nervous system are created from the moment we start moving (even before we are born). As we move, we start to build up networks by linking neurons so that we can produce movement patterns. We can see vast differences in the way that babies move. Babies may have only been moving and creating networks for a year or so. Imagine how different the neurological systems of eight-year-olds will be. So, why would it make sense to make a couple of very different eight-year-olds kick a ball the same way?

Hartley & Laver (2011)

Many multibillion-pound businesses, such as Google, use this principle at the core of their creative process (Robinson, 2010; Brown, 2008). They know that when their people are free to play with ideas, they become creative. The link between play and creativity has been extensively researched within education (Lieberman, 1977). When we are free to play and express ourselves, we become creative (Brown, 2008). Tim Brown (2008), who cites the work of creativity researcher Bob McKim, also notes that when we fear that we will be judged we can become less likely to offer our ideas. We run the risk of embarrassing ourselves in front of our peers. However, when we are engaged in an activity for the simple pleasure of doing it, we will often experiment, try things differently and explore. We use our imagination to help us find new possibilities. This process leads us to finding creative solutions. When we have a trusted environment where there is no judgment or fear of failure, we tend to be more willing to give things a go and see what happens. The more boundaries we have, the less experimentation we tend to do. If you've ever watched young children opening gifts at Christmas, you'll have noticed how much more interesting the box is to them than the gift inside it. Although it seems ironic to adults, to a child the box is far more fascinating. Normally the toy does a few things, but it has a fairly small number of possibilities. The box on the other hand has a vast number of possibilities. A box could be a house, a boat, a cave, a hideout, a store, a plane or just about anything. When you're inside the box your world is a little different. With the box on top of you the world sounds different, looks different and probably smells different. The box becomes fascinating because it has endless possibilities. It engages our natural curiosity, and our imagination starts to give it different meanings (Robinson, 2006, 2010). When these phenomena coincide, our natural creative juices flow. As we play, we try more things. As we try more things, we develop more neural connections. More networks, connections and links in our brain equals more intelligence (Caine & Caine, 1990). With more neural connections and more intelligence, we and our brains can adapt to novel situations more effectively.

None of that happens in our comfort zone.

What happens if you don't operate in an environment that lends itself to creativity? What if your environment is judgmental and rigid? What if there is a very clear definition of 'right', 'wrong', 'good' and 'bad' and you're expected to simply get things 'right'? What if your management environment demands that you get it right every time without fail?

You manage your internal environment (Glasser, 1999). You choose how your internal environment is governed. You have the power to decide whether you push yourself into your discomfort zone or not. You decide whether you let your ego, or the risks of failure, constrict you. Moving into your discomfort zone doesn't mean that you have to revolutionize the world. You don't need to invent the next microchip. It could simply be that you challenge yourself to find better, more efficient or more effective ways to do things. You could challenge yourself to do things at a higher standard, more precisely or more consistently. You could work to improve your skills, techniques, approaches or strategies. Rather than shying away from critical comments, you could seek them out and use them to help you improve. These are all examples of moving beyond your comfort zone. You are the only one who can dictate whether you operate in your comfort zone or your discomfort zone. The simple fact is that if we want to achieve peak performances, we need to operate at the edge of our capabilities (Csikszentmihalyi, 1990). Alistair White's (2009) model, from performance management, shows that the *Optimal Performance Zone* lies outside of the comfort zone.

So, how can we start to embrace our discomfort zone? One answer, that I've found to be particularly helpful, is to start with baby steps. As I often describe it, "Baby steps, then steps, then strides, then leaps". I've noticed that very few people are keen to start with a giant's leap into the discomfort zone. However, they may well be willing to start small and build up.

Imagine walking across a room, blindfolded. The chances are, you're not going to take huge confident strides straightaway. Instead, you'll probably start with tentative little steps. As you become more confident, your stride length will naturally increase, as you learn to trust that the ground in front of you is safe. I've found that it's very similar when we enter our discomfort zone.

As we become more confident in our discomfort zone, we start to shift from enduring it, to enjoying it … and maybe even loving it.

In summary …

- Our discomfort zone is where we learn, grow and improve.
- To love our discomfort zone, we need to embrace and use our mistakes positively.
- To embrace and use our mistakes, we may need to change the way we perceive them.
- To embrace our mistakes, we may need our ego to take a back seat so that we can risk 'failing'.
- Challenge yourself, push yourself and explore new territory.
- Giving up is the reason we fail, not the result of failure.

References

Aronoff, C.E. (2011) *Letting Go: Preparing Yourself to Relinquish Control of the Family Business*, Basingstoke: Palgrave Macmillan.

Bardwick, J. (1995) *Danger in the Comfort Zone: How to Break the Entitlement Habit that's Killing American Business*, New York: American Management Association.

Ben-Shahar, T. (2009) *The Pursuit of Perfect: How to Stop Chasing Perfection and Start Living a Richer, Happier Life*, New York: McGraw Hill Professional.

Brown, T. (2008) 'Tim Brown on creativity and play'. *Keynote Presentation to TED Conference.* 5th November 2008. Online. Available www.ted.com/talks/tim_brown_on_creativity_and_play.html (accessed 31st March 2011).

Caine, R.N. and Caine, G. (1990) 'Understanding a brain-based approach to learning and teaching', *Educational Leadership*, 48(2), 66–70.

Colvin, G. (2008) *Talent is Overrated: What Really Separates World Class Performers from Everybody Else*, New York: Portfolio.

Cotterill, S. and Johnson, P. (2008) 'Exploring the concept of the comfort zone in professional soccer players', *Association for Applied Sport Psychology Annual Conference*. St Louis, USA.

Csikszentmihalyi, M. (1990) *Flow: The Psychology of Optimal Experience*, New York: Harper and Row.

Dayton, G. (2007) 'Trading psychology – The universal law of trading confidence', *Trading Psychology Edge*, September 2007.

Ericsson, K.A. and Charness, N. (1999) 'Expert Performance: It's Structure and Acquisition'. In Williams, W.M. (ed.) *The Nature-Nurture Debate: The Essential Readings*, New York: Wiley.

Gallwey, T. (1986) *The Inner Game of Tennis*, London: Pan Books.

Glasser, W. (1999) *Choice Theory: A New Psychology of Personal Freedom*, New York: Harper Collins.

Halden-Brown, S. (2003) *Mistakes Worth Making: How to turn sports errors into athletic excellence*, Champaign, IL: Human Kinetics.

Hartley, S.R. (2010) 'Learn from everything', *Squash Player*, 38(6), 24.

Hartley, S.R. (2018) *Master Mental Toughness*, Leeds: Be World Class.

Hartley, S.R. and Laver, D.J. (2011) *Street Soccer Coaching*, Somerset, UK: The International Street Soccer Association.

Heath, R. (2009) *Celebrating Failure: The Power of Taking Risks, Making Mistakes and Thinking Big*, New Jersey: Career Press.

Lieberman, J.N. (1977) *Playfulness: Its Relationship to Imagination and Creativity*. New York: Academic Press

Manz, C.C. (2000) *Emotional Discipline: The Power to Choose How You Feel*, San Francisco: Berrett-Koehler.

Manz, C.C. (2002) *The Power of Failure*, San Francisco: Berrett-Koehler.

Metzinger, T. (2010) *The Ego Tunnel: The Science of the Mind and the Myth of the Self*, New York: Basic Books.

Robinson, K. (2006) 'Do schools kill creativity?' *Keynote Presentation to TED Conference*. 26th June 2006. Online. Available www.ted.com/talks/ken_robinson_says_schools_kill_ creativity.html> (accessed 15th December 2010).

Robinson, K. (2010) 'Bring on the learning revolution', *Keynote Presentation to TED Conference*. 24th May 2010. Online. Available www.ted.com/talks/sir_ken_robinson_bring_ on_the_revolution.html> (accessed 15th December 2010).

White, A.A.K. (2009) *From Comfort Zone to Performance Management*, New York: White & MacLean Publishing.

Wolfinger, M.D. (2008) *The Rookies Guide to Options: The Beginner's Handbook of Trading Equity Options*, Cedar Falls, IA: W&A Publishing.

Zander, R.S. and Zander, B. (2000) *The Art Of Possibility: Transforming Professional and Personal Life*, Harvard, MA: Harvard Business School Press.

Release the Hand Brake! **8**

A few years ago, I was working with a long jumper. We were discussing his performance. He was becoming frustrated because he felt that he wasn't jumping freely. He recalled that when he was a little younger, he would charge down the runway for all he was worth and just launch himself into the air. He didn't really have any technique to speak of at the time. In fact, he'd probably have been referred to as a 'raw talent'. However, that seemed to have changed now. He had been working on his technique and was a far more accomplished jumper, in many ways. He was also stronger, faster and more powerful. But he felt as if there was something missing; like he was not quite at full throttle. In the course of our conversation, I asked him, "Do you feel like you're performing with the hand brake on?"

As I looked at other athletes, I saw the same signs. Performers looked like they were performing in some sort of a mental straightjacket. At the time, I wondered if this was specific to athletes. In the case of our long jumper, this might simply have been a symptom of overthinking and the fact that he was concentrating too heavily on his technique (Flegal & Anderson, 2008). Was his mind too full of thoughts to just run and jump? As we talked about it over the course of a few sessions, I started to conclude that *the mental hand brake* is something that exists in many walks of life. It's not restricted to sport.

Most of us probably live life with our hand brake on to a certain extent. We normally hold something back. We keep something in reserve. At times we find ourselves playing within ourselves. It's as if we're scared to show the world all of who we are and what we've got. In short, we don't give fully of ourselves. In the U.K. we would probably see this trait as 'very British'. Is it culturally ingrained? Does it come from the 'stiff upper lip' school of emotional awareness?

DOI: 10.4324/9781003181491-9

I have to admit, I still haven't got to the bottom of this myself. I find myself living my life with the hand brake on at times. I often ask myself what is it that keeps me from dropping my hand brake to the floor and pushing the throttle as far as it will go. Perhaps it is the fear that I will give it everything that I've got and not succeed.

I met a swimmer once who told me that she would never give it everything. She told me that if she kept something in reserve, she could console herself afterwards with the idea that she might have been able to win if she had have given it her all. It was a mental safety net. Her alternative was to know that she'd given it everything and it wasn't good enough. In that situation, she would have no hiding place. She'd have no excuse. She would have to admit that her best wasn't good enough to win (Reitman & Williams, 1961).

Perhaps we use mental hand brakes if we have a fear of success? Fear of success can be just as paralyzing as fear of failure (Miller, 1994). Many people may fear success because it tests their limits and makes them vulnerable to new situations. New challenges are presented, which take us into our discomfort zone. Often success will take us into uncharted territory and break our status quo. Imagine the changes that come when you take a business from sole trader status and start employing people. What happens when you go from a handful of employees to 50, or 100, or more? Imagine all of the new demands. The world will start to change very quickly. You'd have admin, finance, HR and management concerns. You'd be taken out of being a practitioner and become a manager. Although you've always said that you want to run a big business, when it comes to the crunch, do you truly want the things that would go with it? Success could mean a big change (Midgley & Abrams, 1974).

Even worse, success can expose weaknesses and force people to deal with their flaws. Success is scary when it involves change. Success can be intimidating and hard to handle. With success comes more challenge and more responsibilities, which can be threatening. Sometimes people fear success because they don't know if they can live up to their achievements. They don't think they're good enough or smart enough. They're afraid they don't have what it takes to rise to the challenge, and they don't know if they can sustain their success. Psychologist, Roy Baumeister, observed that success can often lead to increased pressure on a performance, and not just increased confidence (Baumeister, Hamilton & Tice, 1985). This often happens when success is public, and performers perceive that there is therefore an increase in expectation. I have seen this a lot in athletes. The athletes believe that if they post a spectacular performance, everyone will expect them to repeat it (Anderson, 2000). The problem is the athlete doesn't know whether they can. Part of them might think it is a fluke. Stuart Dunkel (1989) notes that the same phenomenon is often seen in musicians during the audition process.

Maybe a part of it stems from fear of rejection (Verbeke & Bagozzi, 2000). I can remember my hand brake being firmly on when I was at school. I wasn't enamored with the prospect of approaching girls and asking them out. What if they said 'No'? My poor fragile ego couldn't quite handle the idea. Maybe I felt that if this girl said "No", all the others would probably say "No" as well. Maybe I was scared that if she said "No", I'd lose the only thing I had … the hope. I see the same trait in sales executives often, especially when things aren't going well. Rejections seem to carry the same meaning as they did for me at school.

If this person won't buy, why would the next person (Verbeke and Bagozzi, 2000)?

If I don't ask them, they can't say "No", and I can cling onto the hope.

When we take on this mindset, we often change our behavior. We start avoiding situations. We are torn between wanting to do something but avoiding it because it might lead to rejection. We've probably made a link between rejection and failure (Seaward, 2006). Rejection can hurt (Seaward, 2006). If we think that rejection means that we are not good enough, we're unlikely to put ourselves in a situation where we would experience that … and on comes our hand brake.

Perhaps though, there is another reason. Maybe we are nervous about pushing ourselves to our limit because it takes us to *the edge* (Clash, 2003). How often have we ever been absolutely at the limits of our capability? For most of us, it's unknown territory. We simply don't know what *the edge* is. We don't know what it feels like to be there. It would almost be like stepping onto another planet. What if we couldn't breathe? What if it was too hot? What if our body and mind simply couldn't cope and we blacked out? What if it was just too scary?

There is a distinct possibility that many of us keep the hand brake on because we're scared of losing control (Midgley & Abrams, 1974). When I talk to athletes about releasing the hand brake, we often use the words 'letting go'. Our hand brake gives us control. It stops us from speeding out of control and allows us to do things at a comfortable pace and on our terms. Letting go often means that we must relinquish control. In order to do that we need to trust. The element of our self that has control is our conscious brain, which normally operates under the direction of our ego (Moller, Deci & Ryan, 2006; Baumeister, Heatherton & Tice, 1993). To start releasing our hand brake we need to be confident enough to switch off our conscious brain and allow our unconscious to take over (Gallwey, 1986). Those people who are control freaks, often have the hand brake firmly on.

Let's have a look at the case of our long jumper. We spent a few weeks working on an exercise to help him release his mental hand brake. He found that he was starting to put the brakes on, literally, because he wasn't confident that he could control his speed on the runway. During the winter he'd become faster and more powerful. Running at full pace seemed quite scary to him because it was unfamiliar. It probably felt a little bit like riding down a steep hill on a bike with dodgy brakes. Added to this, he wasn't sure how to control this speed on the take-off board and feared that his technique would be compromised. The result was that he slowed down as he approached the board, rather than accelerating.

We started by making the athlete aware of his hand brake. After a while he could quite accurately tell whether he was running at 70 percent, 80 percent or 100 percent. In fact, he became accurate to within two or three percent. His next challenge was to deliberately control his hand brake. We started experimenting with different speeds of run up. He would try some at 70, some at 85, some at 95, one at 80, one at 100 per. Although his aim was to control the jump as well as possible, there was no success or failure. We were not particularly worried about the outcome of the jump. The point of the exercise was to control the hand brake and become familiar and more comfortable with the hand brake released. Over the course of several weeks, he started to make 85–90 percent jumps consistently in control. This then progressed until he was happy attempting near 100 percent jumps, and eventually controlling them.

Motor racing drivers have a similar mental demand to other elite athletes (Hardcastle, 2008). They need to operate on a knife edge (Clash, 2003). They need to push themselves and the car to the absolute limit of their capability. But it is a fine line. If they overstep the mark, they risk crashing. The consequences of crashing in motor sport could potentially be fatal. However, if they don't push themselves and the car to the limit, they will probably be beaten. If their performance drops by just a percent, it might make the difference between winning and not even scoring a point. For most of us, the prospect would be daunting enough in dry conditions with no other cars on the circuit. Obviously, the challenge increases in a competitive situation with wet tires and spray everywhere.

Do you know where the edge is? Do you know what you are truly capable of? Do you know where your ceiling is? Can you say you have been to the very limit of your capability and given it absolutely everything you had? If so, how did it feel?

The exercise with our long jumper is incredibly simple and can be applied to any walk of life by employing the same process. First, you need to be aware of your hand brake. You need to know whether the hand brake is on fully, and when you've released it slightly. You need to be able to grade it between *fully on* and *fully released*. Once you're aware of this, you can start to deliberately take control and start experimenting. Releasing your hand brake will require challenging yourself on the things which are currently holding you back. You'll need to step into your discomfort zone and start taking on the things that are causing you to pull the hand brake on. You'll need to let go and relinquish control of the things you've been holding onto. You'll have to let go of the things that you've been holding onto for protection.

Do the things that you'd really love to do but don't feel you have the nerve to do.

Dance and don't care what anyone else thinks. So what if they think you look daft? So what if it's not in rhythm?

Sing your heart out and don't care whether it's in tune or not.

Run naked on the beach with the wind in your hair.

I have a few friends that genuinely live life with their hand brake off. They don't tend to show any signs of inhibitions. They don't seem to worry what anyone else will think of them. People who live life with the hand brake off seem to have a far greater sense of freedom. I recently went on a business trip for a week with one particular friend who exemplifies this. I've known this friend most of my adult life, so I'd say I know him pretty well. However, it still surprises me just how enigmatic he can be. Our trip took us to a country that neither of us had been to before. We didn't know anyone, other than our liaison, and we didn't speak a word of the language. Those are not barriers to my friend; they are minor technicalities. They certainly didn't stop my mate engaging everyone he met.

The purpose of our trip was to research the standard of the nation's football and their readiness to qualify for the World Cup. To do this, we needed to understand the current standard of their football across the board, from the kids in the street to the current national team. We turned up one evening at a playground in the middle of the capital. My friend set up some speed testing equipment and got some of the kids who were playing football to come over and do some sprint tests. My mate is a big character, full of energy and he always wears a smile. The kids, of course, took to him immediately. "Who is the fastest?" he said (in English). Within five minutes he'd got kids coming from everywhere to have a go and test themselves. After 20–30 minutes we've found some winners, given out some baseball caps and we have a great set of data.

How many people would just have wandered into a playground full of teenagers in an Arab capital city and started running sprint tests? Most people's fears or uncertainty would probably have started to conjure up all sorts of reasons why they couldn't just get stuck in. They would need an interpreter. They'd need it to be prearranged and organized. My friend didn't need an interpreter. He had a smile. He had that easy self-assured confidence and the natural energy that comes with genuine enthusiasm. That's all he needed. In fact, in most situations, those ingredients tend to work just fine.

So, what is it that gives people this freedom? How can they operate without all the reserves and safeguards that most people use? What is it that allows them to just dive in without the concerns or fears that might cause the rest of us to stutter? Here's one answer …

They *know* themselves … and they are *happy* with themselves … therefore, they can *be* themselves!

Is this an ancient wisdom that most of us have forgotten (Aristotle, trans. 1976; Corlett, 1996)?

Herein lays perhaps the greatest single secret to success in my humble opinion. How many people genuinely know themselves? One of the hardest questions in life is, 'Who are you?' I often ask people that question. Initially, most will answer by telling me their roles, or their labels. They might tell me their name, which is a label. They might tell me their job, or their role within a family. For example, my name is Simon Hartley, I am a husband, a father and a performance coach.

None of those responses tell me who Simon Hartley is. The person that we are endures beyond any life circumstances, such as jobs or family situations. I would not become a different person if I changed my name or stopped being a performance coach. I was not a different person the day before I married or the day before my first daughter was born. I'll admit that there are aspects of me that have changed because of those events, but the core of who I am remains.

Some people will try to go one stage further and add some form of evaluation or judgment to their labels. For example, they might say, "I'm a pretty good husband" or "a very experienced performance coach", or a "successful entrepreneur". However, those are just extensions of our roles and labels. They still don't answer the question, "Who are you?" (Potter, 2010)

In order to get the real answers, we need to look more deeply at ourselves. We can start by becoming self-aware (Bach, 1974), and reflecting on our selves in our lives. We need to look at how we tend to react in various situations, how we think, how we feel in different circumstances, what affects us and what doesn't. Here are some questions that I've used to start the thought process.

When are you kind and helpful? When do you tend not to be? What dictates how kind and helpful you might be?

When are you generous? When do you tend not to be? What dictates how generous you might be?

When are you a good friend? Do you make and break friendships quickly? What would cause you to break off a friendship?

When are you hard working? When do you push yourself hardest? What motivates you and what turns you off completely?

When are you focused? When do you get distracted more easily?

When do you enjoy life the most? When don't you enjoy life?

When are you optimistic and when are you pessimistic?

How do you respond to difficult challenges? How do you respond to knocks? How many times would you take a knock before you gave up? When do knocks hurt you?

How do you respond to criticism? How do you respond to praise? How do you respond to rejection?

When do you find that you let other people get to you, and when do you tend not to be bothered? What would they have to say? Have you got an Achilles heel? If so, what is it?

How do you think of other people? How judgmental are you? What do you tend to be judgmental about? What do you tend to criticize other people for? What do you praise other people for?

In what situations would you feel safe and secure … or threatened and afraid … or happy … or sad … or confident … or nervous … serious … silly … angry … calm .. frustrated … patient … determined … strong and powerful … weak and helpless? Who or what could change your thoughts and emotions? Who could do it and what would they have to do or say?

The answers to these sorts of questions start to build up a picture of who we are. I like to think of myself as a generous person. However, I know that there are limits to my generosity. I tend to be more generous with people close to me and my generosity tends to reflect how affluent I am feeling at the time. I am passionate about helping homeless people, but I don't give all my spare cash to people on the streets as I walk through the city.

We are complex individuals. Very rarely do we follow black-and-white rules. We don't tend to always react one way or another. In order to understand ourselves, we need to know how we think, feel, behave and respond. This will tell us an awful lot about our values and beliefs. For example, how we judge others will tell us a lot about how we judge ourselves and about what we believe is important. For example, do we judge other people by their body-fat percentage? If so, we're probably not going to be too proud about our own flabby bits and we'll work hard to cover them up. If we judge being fat as 'bad', we'll have a negative view of our self if we feel that we're overweight. We're unlikely to be comfortable in the nude. We won't want to show the world who we are, in all our glory, because there are bits of us we're ashamed of (Potter, 2010).

Do we make judgments about people based on their finances? Do we judge people by the car they drive, the clothes they wear or the house they live in? If so, we're likely to judge ourselves in the same way. We're likely to be ashamed if we drive a ten-year-old car that's looking the worse for wear. Would we proudly drive up to the entrance in it or sheepishly park it around the corner and walk? How will we feel about ourselves when we're driving it? If we feel that making money is an outward sign of success, will we judge that this car is a symbol of our failure?

Deeper self-knowledge requires us to answer some of the more fundamental questions. Self-knowledge focuses on knowing who we are; our values, what we stand for, our deepest beliefs (Nesti, 2004; Valle & Halling, 1989).

If we believe that we're not what we want to be, we won't be happy being ourselves. Why would you be yourself, if you weren't happy with who you were? By being yourself, you'd allow the world to see who you are. If you aren't happy with yourself, you won't be yourself. Instead, your ego will try to create an image of the person you want to be, and project that to the world (Metzinger, 2010; Epstein, 2006). If you're not happy being yourself, your ego will start trying to portray a different you. It will try to hide your 'faults'. It will try to create a mask and a facade. It will put on a brave face when things are going badly. Your ego will criticize other people openly, to demonstrate how different to them you are. It will look to pull others down to make yourself appear greater. Ultimately, if we don't believe that our 'self' is good enough, we won't be happy with it and we won't present it to the world (Chopra, Williamson & Ford, 2010).

When we find ourselves in that pattern, we are living life with the hand brake on! We're reserved and guarded. We are trying to be someone we're not, which takes a great deal of effort. It is not free and effortless. It is defensive. We end up being governed by what we imagine others will think of us. Our mind is so tied up being concerned with our image, it's not free to just *be* (Bach, 1974; Vajda, 2008).

I think it all comes back to how we define success (Frankl, 1959/1984). Our ego tries desperately to make us appear successful in whatever we believe is important. If we're in business, our ego wants the world to see that we're a great business person. If we're an athlete, the ego wants to show the world what a great athlete we are. The criteria for success are therefore set out for us. If it's business, the criteria might be money. In sport, it could be a ranking, medal haul, number of caps for your country, grand slam wins, records, or championship titles.

What if we changed our definition of success? What if success meant being our self and being true to our self?

Socrates would probably argue that being your self is *the* number one goal in life (Aristotle, trans. 1976). Everything else is secondary. If we made loads of money but were not our self, in Socrates' eyes that would constitute failure. If we won 50 Olympic Gold medals and we failed to be our self, it could also be argued that we'd missed the point. In fact, it could also be argued that we'd worked so hard to make the money or win the medals so that we wouldn't need to be our self. Instead of being our self, we could then hide behind the money or the medals and try to convince our self we had been successful. Whatever other failings we may have, we could console our self by focusing on the money or the medals and pretend all was well.

What if we swapped our priorities? What if we decided that being our self *was* success? What if our aim in any given task or situation was to understand our self and be our self (May, 1953)? Life has a way of challenging us in everything we do. Situations will tempt you away from being your self in some way. We might be tempted away by the prospect of money, reward, fame, or recognition. Equally, we might be driven by the fear of being exposed, embarrassed, ridiculed, or humiliated (Vajda, 2008). Whatever the situation, Socrates would probably say that our job was simply to be authentic and true to our self. These are profound concepts that have been at the center of philosophy for centuries (Hatzomoysis, 2010). I would argue that they are also central to our lives every day (May, 1953).

I remember having a conversation with my Ph.D. tutor. It was while I was working in Premier League football. I was in a culture that didn't match any of my values. Players didn't want to be the best that they could be. It was not a culture of excellence; it was a culture of excuses. Rather than working hard to turn around their performance, the players backed away. At the helm was a manager who was rude and disrespectful. I felt completely out of place. I felt like an ice cube in boiling water. At one point it struck me that I had two choices; either change myself to become part of the culture or leave. It was a highly paid job at the pinnacle of my profession. I'd worked all my professional life to get to that point. The choice was easy. I left.

A few years later I found myself having a similar conversation with that very same friend. I was working as an Executive Director in a fast-start business, under a CEO whose vision, values and messages were changing. We started the business with an agreed set of values. But those values had started disintegrating. At one point I remarked that the goal posts had moved so far, I wasn't quite sure I was on the same pitch anymore, or even playing the same sport. I could see parallels developing with my experience in the football club and said to my friend, "If it's a choice between changing my job, or changing myself, I'll be changing the job". A little while later, I left.

I believe that being your self is central to living life with the hand brake off. Once we can start to live and perform with the hand break off, we give ourselves a fighting chance of performing at our peak. If we leave the hand brake on, we stand very little chance. Many people assume that the best way to go faster is to push the throttle. Let's be honest, we can push the throttle all we like, but if we've got the brakes on, we're not going to get far. With brakes on and throttle to the floor, we'll just create friction and eventually burn out the engine. If we let the brakes off first, we could even switch off the engine and freewheel downhill with effortless speed.

In summary …

- Often our ego causes us to live our life with the hand brake on.
- Know your self. Understand who you are, not the labels that describe what you do.
- Be yourself.
- Be happy with yourself.
- Does it really matter what everyone else thinks?
- Review your definition of success. Perhaps success *is* being yourself.

References

Anderson, M. (2000) *Doing Sport Psychology*, Champaign, IL: Human Kinetics.

Aristotle (trans). 1976) *The Nicomachean Ethics ('Ethics')*, Harmondsworth: Penguin.

Bach, K. (1974) *Exit Existentialism: A Philosophy of Self-Awareness*, Florence, KY: Wadsworth Publishing.

Baumeister, R.F., Hamilton, J.C. and Tice, D.M. (1985) 'Public versus private expectancy of success: Confidence booster or performance pressure?', *Journal of Personality and Social Psychology*, 48(6), 1447–1457.

Baumeister, R.F., Heatherton, T.F. and Tice, D.M. (1993) 'When ego threats lead to self-regulation failure: Negative consequences of high self-esteem', *Journal of Personality and Social Psychology*, 64(1), 141–156.

Chopra, D., Williamson, M. and Ford, D (2010) *The Shadow Effect: Illuminating the Hidden Power of Your True Self*, New York: HarperOne.

Clash, M.J. (2003) *Forbes to the Limits: Pushing Yourself to the Edge in Adventure and in Business*, New York: Wiley.

Corlett, J. (1996) 'Sophistry, Socrates and sport psychology', *The Sport Psychologist*, 10(1), 84–94.

Dunkel, S.E. (1989) *The Audition Process: Anxiety Management and Coping Strategies*, Hillside, NY: Pendragon Press.

Epstein, J. (2006) *The Little Book on Big Ego: A Guide to Manage and Control the Egomaniacs in Your Life*, New York: Alnola Productions Inc.

Flegal, K. and Anderson, M. (2008) 'Overthinking skilled motor performance', *Psychonomic Bulletin & Review*, 15, 927–932.

Frankl, V.E. (1959/1984) *Man's Search for Meaning*, New York: Touchstone.

Gallwey, T. (1986) *The Inner Game of Tennis*, London: Pan Books.

Hardcastle, P. (2008) *Psychology of Motorsport Success: How to Improve Your Performance with Mental Skills Training*, Somerset, UK: J.H. Haynes & Co. Ltd.

Hatzomoysis, A. (2010) *Self-Knowledge*, New York: Oxford University Press USA.

May, R. (1953) *Man's Search for Himself*, New York: W.W. Norton & Co.

Metzinger, T. (2010) *The Ego Tunnel: The Science of the Mind and the Myth of the Self*, New York: Basic Books.

Midgley, N. and Abrams, M.S. (1974) 'Fear of success and locus of control in young women', *Journal of Consulting and Clinical Psychology*, 42(5), 737.

Miller, J.R. (1994) 'Fear of success: Psychodynamic implications', *Journal of American Academy of Psychoanalysis*, 22,129–136.

Moller, A.C., Deci, E.L. and Ryan, R.M. (2006) 'Choice and ego-depletion: The moderating role of autonomy', *Personality and Social Psychology Bulletin*, 32(8), 1024–1036.

Nesti, M.S. (2004) *Existential Psychology and Sport: Theory and Application*, Oxford: Routledge.

Potter, A. (2010) *The Authenticity Hoax: How We Get Lost Finding Ourselves*, New York: Harper.

Reitman, E.E. and Williams, C.D. (1961) 'Relationships between hope of success and fear of failure, anxiety, and need for achievement', *The Journal of Abnormal and Social Psychology*, 62(2), 465–467.

Seaward, B.L. (2006) *Managing Stress: Principles and Strategies for Health and Wellbeing*, Sudbury, MA: Jones & Bartlett Publishing.

Vajda, P.D. (2008) *Why Being Authentic is so Difficult*, Atlanta, GA: Spirit Heart.

Valle, R. and Halling, S. (1989) *Existential-Phenomenological Perspectives in Psychology: Exploring the Breadth of Human Experience*, New York: Plenum Press.

Verbeke, W. and Bagozzi, R.P. (2000) 'Sales call anxiety: Exploring what it means when fear rules a sales encounter', *Journal of Marketing*, 64(3), 88–101.

Avoid the Trapdoors　　　9

> "Life is simple, but we insist on making it complicated".
>
> Confucius (a long time ago)

Sport, business and life are actually pretty simple when we strip them back to the basics. If we took everything on its own merit, our lives would be a doddle. However, as human beings, we have a tendency to confuse everything. We add a lot of garbage into the mix, and we often lose sight of the simple task in front of us. We take a molehill and turn it into a mountain.

How difficult is it really to sink a three-foot putt? If you're not a golfer, it might be a challenge. If you've practiced putting for years, should be relatively easy (Fisher, 1998).

How difficult is it to deliver a sales pitch? If you're not a sales executive, it might be a challenge. If you've been selling all your life, it's pretty straightforward.

How is it possible then that a golfer could feel nervous standing over a three-foot putt? What if we put a gun to their head and told them that we'd shoot them if they missed? Would that change the task? Would the challenge suddenly change from sinking a putt to saving a life? What if we had a big red button instead? If the golfer misses the putt, we will press the big red button and detonate the Earth. Does the challenge now change from sinking a putt to saving the world? .. or is it still a three-foot putt? (Fisher, 1998).

If the golfer thinks that the challenge is to save the Earth, he'll probably see that as a tough one. He may not have saved the world before, so there is a chance that he'll see it as impossible. All of a sudden, the three-foot putt starts to take on a new meaning. We've complicated the very simple task and turned it into a monster. Our little molehill just became a mountain. All too often we do exactly the same things in our lives. The example of the golfer

DOI: 10.4324/9781003181491-10

saving the world is perhaps a little extreme, but we have a habit of applying the same process to many simple tasks. When we do this, we start to create trapdoors for ourselves. These trapdoors are scattered in our path as we try to navigate through our lives. Most people are unaware of them, until they step on one and start to experience the sensation of falling. Before they know what's happened, they are struggling to perform things that should be simple for them. They're so caught up in the negative spiral, the pressure and the anxiety, they almost forget how to perform. In gymnastics there is a condition that is known as 'lost move syndrome' (Day, Thatcher, Greenlees & Woods, 2006). It refers to a phenomenon where the gymnast will simply not be able to execute a move that they have done hundreds of times before.

A few years ago, I worked with a gymnast. He was a Great Britain international and specialized in the trampoline. He had developed 'lost move syndrome' for one move in particular but noticed that it was starting to affect other moves as well. When we started talking, it became apparent that it was a symptom of overthinking. As he took off, his mind started asking, 'what if …?'. Initially he asked, 'What if I don't land on the cross?' Over time this evolved into, 'What if I don't land properly and I hurt myself?' As you can imagine, things happen very quickly when the gymnast is in the air. There really isn't time for a conversation in your mind. The window to exit the somersault lasts for a split second and the gymnast has to time it just right. There is no way that the thinking brain can find that point because it flashes past too quickly. The subconscious, nonthinking brain finds it no problem. So, imagine how scary it would be to try to perform the skill with your thinking brain. Imagine how hard it would be to *consciously* get your timing exactly right. Even to an experienced gymnast, that is a near impossible task. The only way to perform the skill (and find the perfect exit point) is to trust; allow the nonthinking brain to perform naturally as it has done hundreds of times before (Gallwey, 1986).

So, what is it that caused our gymnast to start thinking? Let's have a look at the start of the 'what ifs …?' It all started because the athlete was concerned that he might not hit the cross perfectly. The cross on the trampoline is there for good reason. It's right in the center and therefore gives the gymnast the best take-off for the next move. If he'd missed the cross a few times and found the next few moves more difficult, it may have affected his routine. So, how does that suddenly become 'lost move syndrome', not just in one move but in a number of different moves?

The answer is that our gymnast fell down a trapdoor. Hitting the cross started to become an issue because it had an impact on the result. Our gymnast started to get caught up in the outcome and therefore started overthinking. He started getting sucked into the negative spiral that we discussed in the Introduction

(Lindsley, Brass & Thomas, 1995). He made a mistake, started to analyze, to overthink, and therefore he produced another mistake. If you remember back to the performance spirals, this leads to a compound effect. The mistakes get bigger. On the trampoline, when mistakes become too big, you risk injury.

We all create our own trapdoors. Normally, they are created because we are tying ourselves to the results and the outcome in some way. We've started to overcomplicate our simple task by adding an outcome to it. When we do that, we run the risk of perceiving that the outcome lies beyond our capability. We set ourselves an impossible task. In the case of our gymnast, we need to start dismantling the trapdoor. We need to understand why the outcome has so much importance to him. We need to allow him to see the task for what it is. His job is not to save the world, it is to execute a skill that he's done hundreds of times before. He doesn't have to do it perfectly. He has to execute it to the best of his ability. With practice, his best will be better next week than it is today and even better in a few weeks' time.

Our gymnast had actually fallen down a trapdoor that many people create for themselves. He'd started to link his success on the trampoline to success in life. Trampolining had taken on an artificial level of importance. All of a sudden, this move was not just a move anymore. The routine was not just a linked series of moves that he could execute in his sleep. Instead, it constituted a huge proportion of his self-worth. His performance on the trampoline was being used as a measure of his success as a person. Success in sport had started to equal success in life. That is a very dangerous place to be. In that situation, we start to pin all of our self-worth to the performance. If we screw up the performance, we are nothing (Covington, 1984; Covington, 1992).

Here's an excerpt from a session with an elite junior rower.

> We talked for quite a while about your reasons for rowing. I'm always keen to really challenge an athlete's reasons for doing what they do – it's a kind of stress-test. You said that getting good scores and being successful is a big reason to row. Like many athletes, there is not much time left in your life (after rowing and school) for a lot else. So, rowing plays a big part in your life. The potential danger with this is that if everything (your happiness in life, feeling successful etc.) hinges on success in rowing, you create a great deal of pressure on yourself to perform. You start to see that if rowing goes wrong, life goes wrong, because rowing is so important to you. This is a pretty fragile position to be in!

Does that mean that we shouldn't want success? Surely that can't be right. In Chapter 5, we said that motivation is underpinned by 'really wanting something'. However, it can be a double-edged sword, especially if *want* turns into *need*. Here's another piece from a summary report that I wrote for an elite junior football player.

> There is always an 'up' side and a 'down' side to *wanting it*. When you're on the field, you need to have the desire to win the ball, get to it first, stay strong in the challenge etc. However, a lot of players start to worry what will happen if they don't succeed. A lot of players have a fear of losing what they have or what they dream of having. If you've got fear, you're screwed. Watch *Star Wars: Episode III* if you get a chance and listen to Yoda talking to Anakin Skywalker about why fear of losing something is always going to screw you up. Yoda warns Anakin against looking into the future. He explains that fear of loss is the path to the dark side and that attachment has its dangers. Finally, Yoda says, 'train yourself to let go of everything you fear to lose'.
>
> To get around this, I think it's really important to have a great safety net. What if you weren't playing football? What would you do if you were injured, and the doc told you that you'd never play again? You have to be happy with a future where you weren't playing pro football. If you know you have a great future with or without football, you'll not have that fear of losing it.

Interestingly, philosophers Kevin Decker and Eberl (2005) also use the film *Star Wars* to illustrate that lack of self-knowledge leads to loss of self-control and anxiety.

Working with an elite junior fencer recently has given me perhaps the most striking example (excuse the pun).

The fencer trains and competes as part of an elite squad that is based regionally. He is one of the top two or three in the country in his age group and discipline. As with most elite athletes, he spends a lot of time fencing. His world is largely made up of fencing. His friends are fencers. His social life is fencing. Whenever he's not at school he is training or competing. As with many other athletes, life *is* fencing. The people that form his immediate society all live and breathe fencing too. Fencing is therefore incredibly important to them as well. As a result, fencing starts to take on a different and artificial meaning. It now becomes a means of creating a social standing. Rankings start to become the basis on which the social hierarchy is formed. It is almost like a monetary currency. As you can imagine, all this baggage starts to form the trapdoor for the fencer. It becomes important to win so that he can maintain his social standing. He gets frustrated and angry if he starts losing points to lower-ranked opponents. He loses sight of the task in front of him and starts focusing on the spectators. Fencing could be easy. It could simply be a case of trying to hit the opponent before the opponent hits you. On the other hand, it could be a mission to become an important, recognized person and gain the respect of a community. Clark Sorensen (1994) found the same patterns within education, in situations where academic achievement is closely linked with social class.

In our example, fencing is being used as a way of establishing and confirming self-worth. Poor performance equals low self-worth. Losing equals low self-worth. I think we've just found a trapdoor.

> "A gold medal is a wonderful thing, but if you're not enough without it, you'll never be enough with it".
>
> Irv Blitzer (John Candy), from the film *Cool Runnings*

This situation is very true in business environments, medical environments, local politics and general life too. Martin Covington (1992) has studied the same phenomena in education. I've seen the same with sales teams. I've seen it within boardrooms and executive teams. When I was younger, I saw it in the local Scouting Association. I saw people's self-worth tied to their title. Grown adults were scrabbling to become the next 'Assistant District Commissioner' because it gave them some social standing.

This all becomes exacerbated if we start to hype up our performances. How often have you seen people talk themselves up, and then crumble under the 'pressure' to then deliver (Baumeister, Hamilton & Tice, 1985)? It happens with colleagues in businesses, elite athletes and even mates playing a round on the golf course. Our friend the ego is in the driving seat as usual and starts to create our trapdoors for us. There are fantastic illustrations in the media. TV shows such as *The Apprentice* are prime examples. Sports such as boxing and football are also characterized by ego-fueled media hype, which can also create trapdoors for performers.

In the last chapter we discussed the role that our ego plays. Our ego is concerned with our image and our identity (Lapsley & Power, 1988). To make the ego's life easier, it starts to apply all sorts of labels to help us identify our self. A lot of athletes associate themselves very strongly with their labels. Academics often refer to 'athletic identity', because a lot of sports people identify themselves so closely with their sport (Sparkes, 1998). We often do this when the activity that we're identifying ourselves with is important to us. I once played cricket. I was absolutely garbage. My highest score ever was three not-out. I once bowled an over with eight wides. I never referred to myself as 'a cricketer', because being good at cricket never held any importance to me. It was something I did on a Sunday with my college mates and nothing more. However, when I was at college, I did refer to myself as 'a rugby player'. I spent a lot of time training, playing, and helping run the student team. Therefore, it made up a large part of my identity.

Although adopting an identity is something we naturally do, it can also cause us to create trapdoors. We usually start applying a judgment in addition to the identity. We'll start by saying, 'I am a sales executive' (for example). However, that's not usually enough for our ego. Our ego would like to think of itself as *good*. So, we set ourselves a target of being a good sales executive. The problem is, when we're not selling very much, our ego could conclude that we're a 'bad' sales executive. If being a sales executive is important to our identity, and being 'good' is important to us, we're in a vulnerable position if it goes wrong. If we hadn't aligned ourselves strongly with that identity, we would probably not have worried too much if we were not selling. I wasn't particularly worried that I only scored three runs and never took a wicket on the cricket field because I didn't consider myself to be 'a cricketer'.

Perhaps the solution is to have a broad sense of identity. If your identity hinges on one thing, you will tend to place a great deal of pressure on that thing (Symes, 2010). In this scenario, your identity is dependent on your success. If you have a wide range of things with which you identify yourself, you'll be able to take a more measured view. But how does that work for an athlete who spends most of their waking life focused on their sport? How does it work for an entrepreneur that spends 16–18 hours a day working on their business? What else can they focus on?

In the last chapter we discussed the importance of knowing yourself. As we said, our roles and labels change. They are situational. At the age of 65, the likelihood is that the 'athlete' will not be an athlete anymore. At the age of 85, the entrepreneur may not be in business. Therefore, maybe we should identify ourselves with who we are, rather than our roles. Perhaps we should ensure that our sense of self-worth is governed by how we live our lives, not on our sales performance, the turnover of the business, our titles, or our ranking (May, 1953). Some athletes face a major challenge when they come to the end of their competitive career (Grove, Lavallee & Gordon, 1997). Most athletes have held a strong connection with their athletic identity since they were small. All of a sudden, their identity is questioned. If they're no longer an athlete … who are they? It is often the same for other people as they retire. If they are not the CEO of the company … who are they? People with a broad sense of self find that they answer those questions much more easily. Their *self* is not dependent upon one particular thing, and they don't need success in a specific field in order to find self-worth.

A little while ago, I worked with a middle-distance runner who was really struggling. He had been injured for a prolonged period and his physiotherapist was concerned that there were other issues starting to develop. The athlete was finding it hard being 'an athlete' who wasn't running. Running was his life and being an athlete was his identity. His athletics gave him a sense of pride. Now that he couldn't train or compete, that source of pride had dried up. As a result, the athlete had found himself caught in a downward spiral.

The lack of pride meant that he didn't really like himself very much. Because he didn't like himself very much, he didn't treat himself very well. He wasn't eating well so he felt tired and lethargic. His body was therefore slower to heal. The knock-on effect was that he became unmotivated and viewed himself as lazy. He couldn't work out why he was being lazy because he values hard work and achievement. As a person that places importance on hard work, laziness is not something he enjoyed viewing himself as. Therefore, he didn't like himself very much, and the spiral continued.

The athlete needed to break the cycle. The solution was simply to start liking himself again. But he could not use his training and competition performances as fuel. In fact, he could not use athletics or his identity as an athlete. Therefore, he had to start looking at himself in other ways. I asked him what he valued in people. He came up with around eight things, including 'hard working', 'kind, self-less and helpful', 'generous' and 'comfortable and happy with themselves'. I then asked him how his friends would describe him in those terms. How hard working would they say he was? How generous, how helpful, and how self-less? We started to create a picture of how he felt he was viewed by those who knew him best, and how he viewed himself. Typically, he viewed himself more modestly than he felt others would view him. Nevertheless, we started to broaden his sense of self. Of course, there were elements that he didn't think were perfect, so we set out to help him improve on those areas. Gradually he began to focus on his true self, rather than his narrow athletic identity. He also developed the areas of himself that he wished to improve. As a result, he was able to be happy with himself as a person, not just as an athlete (Nesti, 2004).

The process that our runner went through did not happen overnight. I genuinely believe that significant changes take time and effort. I often use the phrase, 'real change requires real changes' when I'm working with people. For many people, the process can be pretty uncomfortable (Nesti, 2004). We often need to take a real hard look at ourselves and start to ask some serious questions. We need to address things that we've previously put off, brushed under the carpet, or chosen to overlook. I tend to refer to this process as 'turning out our boxes'.

Imagine an attic full of boxes. The boxes typically contain our memories. We have accumulated them throughout our lives. They normally have trinkets, photo albums or old letters and cards. When it comes to physical objects, we normally tend to keep the nice things or the things which we want to have around us and want to remember. Whenever I've moved house, it always seems to take two or three times as long as it should because we end up finding all of the photo albums and scrapbooks, which we reminisce over.

The same thing happens in our minds. We accumulate memories and experiences and store them away. This is referred to as the personal unconscious within psychology (Jung, 1968). Some of these memories and experiences might be positive, others will be negative. However, we don't often choose whether we keep hold of them or throw them out. Normally, we keep them all, especially the ones that are associated with powerful emotions. For example, an experience that came with a deep feeling of guilt will tend to stay with us. As a result, we have a mental attic full of boxes. Some of those boxes contain things we don't really like, or don't want to look at (Nesti, 2004; Bach, 1974). We try to fool ourselves into thinking that if we ignore them, they will go away. Perhaps if we just keep doing what we do each day, they'll magically resolve themselves. Hopefully, we'll never have to open up those boxes and actually sort them out.

Unfortunately, the reality tends to be different. Innately we all know that we're the only ones that can actually sort out our mental attic. Experience may also tell us that if we don't sort out the boxes ourselves, the contents will tend to jump out on us at some critical moment. It always happens at the very point we least want it to. Those nasty horrible things that we've been avoiding often present themselves in situations of high emotion. Inevitably, when we feel under most pressure or we're anxious about something; our little boxes become trapdoors. Sometimes the boxes can contain powerful negative memories that we've been locking away. These in particular can almost become like explosive trapdoors, or land mines.

In my experience, there is only one solution. We need to pull out the boxes, open them up and start to address and resolve whatever is inside them (Allione, 2008; Epstein, 1995). So far, I've found that the vast majority of issues center around three elements – fear, anger and guilt. These tend to be the issues we need to resolve. We need to forgive ourselves for whatever we feel guilty about or forgive others for whatever we feel angry about. We need to conquer whatever fears we have. Normally this involves some discomfort and usually takes courage (Gilbert, 2005). Usually, it will involve admitting that we were wrong or accepting parts of our character that we might wish were different. It is our ego and our pride that feel the discomfort. They are the aspects of our self that probably caused the issues in the first place. It is likely to have been our ego that felt guilty, angry or fearful, which we subsequently locked up in the boxes of our mental attic.

There is one huge benefit that we receive once we have cleared out our boxes. The process demands that we take responsibility (Martin Fischer & Ravizza, 1998). If we are to truly resolve any of these issues, we must take responsibility. If we blamed someone else, we would simply not get to a point of resolution. Instead, we would simply be resealing the box (with all the nasty stuff still inside it) and putting it back in the attic. We stand the very real chance that we'd worsen the issue and make it all potentially more explosive by adding 'blame' into the mix. Blame tends to increase anger or guilt, rather than reduce it. These concepts are central to many methods used in psychotherapy (Sommers-Flanagan & Sommers-Flanagan, 2004)

By taking responsibility when we clear out our boxes, we start a process of taking responsibility as we go forwards. If we take responsibility and avoid blaming circumstances or other people, we will avoid creating new boxes and new trapdoors in the future. If we blame others or blame circumstance, we hand over control of our destiny. Only when we take responsibility, can we take control (Jauncey, 2002; Koestenbaum & Block, 2001; Martin Fischer & Ravizza, 1998; Nesti, 2004). It is a fundamental element of producing peak performances. It is a trait that is common among true champions. Taking responsibility is a habit of the great performers.

In summary …

- Take things at their own merit and see them for what they really are.
- Ensure that you have a broad and balanced life.
- Performance in one area does not dictate your success as a person.
- Our ego tends to create trapdoors. If we can put ego to bed, the trapdoors tend to disappear.
- Sometimes we need to confront the things that are uncomfortable.

References

Allione, T. (2008) *Feeding the Demons: Ancient Wisdom for Resolving Inner Conflict*, London: Little, Brown & Co.

Bach, K. (1974) *Exit Existentialism: A Philosophy of Self-Awareness*, Florence, KY: Wadsworth Publishing.

Baumeister, R.F., Hamilton, J.C. and Tice, D.M. (1985) 'Public versus private expectancy of success: Confidence booster or performance pressure?', *Journal of Personality and Social Psychology*, 48(6), 1447–1457.

Covington, M.V. (1984) 'The self-worth theory of achievement motivation: Findings and implications', *Elementary School Journal*, 85(1), 5–20.

Covington, M.V. (1992) *Making the Grade: A Self-Worth Perspective on Motivation and School Reform*, Cambridge: Cambridge University Press.

Day, M.C., Thatcher, J., Greenlees, I. and Woods, B. (2006) 'The causes of and psychological responses to lost move syndrome in national level trampolinists', *Journal of Applied Sport Psychology*, 18, 151–166.

Decker, K.S. and Eberl, J.T. (2005) *Star Wars and Philosophy: More Powerful Than You Can Possibly Imagine*, Peru, IL: Carus Publishing.

Epstein, M. (1995) *Thoughts Without a Thinker: Psychotherapy from a Buddhist Perspective*, New York: Basic Books.

Fisher, M. (1998) *The Golfer and the Millionaire*, New York: Cassell Illustrated.

Gallwey, T. (1986) *The Inner Game of Tennis*, London: Pan Books.

Gallwey, T. (2003) *The Inner Game of Work*, New York: Texere Publishing.

Gilbert, J. (2005) 'Self-knowledge is the pre-requisite of humanity: Personal development and self-awareness in aid workers', *Development in Practice*, 15(1), 64–69.

Grove, J.R., Lavallee, D. and Gordon, S. (1997) 'Coping with retirement from sport: The influence of athletic identity', *Journal of Applied Sport Psychology*, 9, 191–203.

Jauncey, P. (2002) *Managing Yourself and Others*, Brisbane: CopyRight Publishing.

Jung, C.G. (1968) *Collected Works of C.G. Jung, Vol. 9, Part 1. 2nd ed.*, New York: Princeton University Press.

Koestenbaum, P. and Block, P. (2001) *Freedom and Accountability at Work: Applying Philosophic Insight to the Real World*, New York: Jossey Bass.

Lapsley, D.K. and Power, F.C. (1988) *Self, Ego, and Identity: Integrative Approaches*, New York: Springer.

Lindsley, D.H., Brass, D.J. and Thomas, J.B. (1995) 'Efficacy-Performance spirals: A multilevel perspective', *Academy of Management Review*, 20(3), 645–678.

Martin Fischer, J. and Ravizza, M. (1998) *Responsibility and Control: A Theory of Moral Responsibility*, Cambridge: Cambridge University Press.

May, R. (1953) *Man's Search for Himself*, New York: W.W. Norton & Co.

Nesti, M.S. (2004) *Existential Psychology and Sport: Theory and Application*, Oxford: Routledge.

Sommers-Flanagan, J. and Sommers-Flanagan, R. (2004) 'Existential Theory and Therapy'. In Sommers-Flanagan, J. and Sommers-Flanagan, R. *Counseling and Psychotherapy Theories in Context and Practice: Skills, Strategies and Techniques*. New York: Wiley, pp. 138–173.

Sorensen, C.W. (1994) 'Success and education in South Korea', *Comparative Education Review*, 38(1), 10–35.

Sparkes, A.C. (1998) 'Athletic identity: An Achilles' heel to the survival of self', *Qualitative Health Research*, 8(5), 644–664.

Symes, R. (2010) 'Understanding athletic identity: 'Who am I?'', *Podium Sports Journal*. 24th May 2010. Online. Available www.podiumsportsjournal.com/2010/05/24/understanding-athletic-identity-who-am-i/ (accessed 15th December 2010).

Habits of Great Performers   **10**

Great performers know that great performances don't happen by chance. They don't happen overnight and they can't be produced by the click of a finger. In his book, *Outliers*, Malcolm Gladwell (2008) explains that it takes over 10,000 hours of practice to become expert in something. Malcolm Gladwell cites a number of examples, such as Mozart, the Beatles and Michael Phelps. However, the '10,000-hour rule' as it has been dubbed, could be applied to just about anything.

The 10,000 hour rule also supports the very-well-recognized idea that talent is actually a very poor predictor of performance. It aligns closely with Carol Dweck's ideas around 'growth mindset' and 'fixed mindset' (Dweck, 2007). She found that innate natural ability is also a poor predictor of success in education. Her research showed that it wasn't the most intelligent students that achieved the highest grades, it was those with a work ethic and a desire to improve. Geoff Colvin (2008) wrote an entire book on the subject, which is titled, *Talent is Overrated*. I found exactly the same when I studied world class performers (Hartley, 2012).

To me, the word 'talent' refers to someone's natural gifts. For example, in sport, a talented youngster probably finds the sport easier. They pick up skills faster and take to it more naturally. Their natural gifts give them a start point. The talent gives them potential, but it does not guarantee that they will fulfill that potential (Farrow, Baker & MacMahon, 2007; Starkes & Ericsson 2003). Great performers may have talent, but they certainly don't rely on their talent. Over the last 25 years, I have worked with hundreds of athletes and players. Those athletes who were the most naturally gifted and talented are *not* the ones that have achieved the most. One of the Premier League football clubs I worked with had three exceptionally skilled players. In many people's opinion, two of them were among the most talented that they'd ever seen.

DOI: 10.4324/9781003181491-11

Interestingly, neither of them had any kind of work ethic. Both players relied on their talent to get by. I suspect that their talent had been good enough to get them to that point (i.e., it had been enough to get them into a Premier League club). They hadn't needed to work particularly hard or stretch themselves, so they probably didn't see any need to change. Despite their talents, both players found it difficult to make a real impression or secure a regular first team slot. They regularly found themselves coming off the substitute's bench. Occasionally they would produce a moment of extreme skill, but rarely did they make a significant impact. One of the players was simply not physically fit enough (and wouldn't work hard enough to become fit). Therefore, he couldn't make a sustained impression on the games. Eventually, both players ended up leaving the club. They played in and around the top flight for a season or two but then disappeared. Arguably, neither of them realized their potential or made the most of their talent.

In comparison, there was a *no-frills* central defender at the club who was, by his own admission, not the most talented footballer on Earth. He was an extremely good professional. He worked hard and was very diligent about his game. Although not supremely talented, he has absolutely made the most of the talent he had. Arguably, he did realize his potential. Unlike the two naturally gifted players, our hard-working professional played Premier League football for many years.

I saw a very similar situation when working in Premiership rugby union. Our club had two fly-halves, both of whom were excellent players. Our first-choice player was very professional. He worked incredibly hard at his game and was constantly looking for ways to improve. He would often be seen taking a bag of balls out of his car boot when everyone else was heading home after training. As many other players were hitting the golf course, or switching on their PlayStations, he would be practicing. He would be in the gym early, sometimes on his own with the fitness trainer, and was often last to leave.

Our second-choice fly-half was not lazy by any means. He did what he was asked to do and didn't cut corners. He was also arguably the more naturally talented of the two. However, he wasn't the first choice in his position. As a result, he was often played out of position. Eventually he chose to leave the club in an attempt to become a first-choice fly-half somewhere else. In truth, our first-choice fly-half closed the talent gap between himself and his teammate with sheer hard work.

These are not isolated examples. I'm sure you've seen many similar situations yourself. It is often the person, or team, that is willing to go the extra mile that will be the most successful. There are some who will disregard the tiny details, thinking they are unimportant or won't make any difference. Others will make sure they pick up on the tiny details and get them absolutely right. Many years ago, I met a former Course Fishing World Champion. I listened to him explaining why one person can catch loads of fish, while the person sitting next to them catches almost nothing. He explained that there were a number of tiny details, that only made a minute difference. In fact, there were a couple of dozen minute things that made a difference. For example, how neatly the hooks were tied, how thick the line was, how clean the bait was, how accurately the bait was presented to the fish. All these tiny details added up. The cumulative effect was that the fish would tend to choose one angler's bait over the other. The tiny details made the difference between winning a World Championship and not winning.

I often listen to the Performance Directors from Olympic sports talking about how they plan to gain a competitive advantage over the opposition. On one occasion, I listened to Stephen Park, the Olympic Manager from the RYA (British Sailing team) explaining how the polish that they applied to the bottoms of the boats made a slight difference to the drag on the boat. The cost of finding, testing, and sourcing the polish was considerable. The effect may have been relatively small, but nonetheless, it was a detail he was determined to get right. I know that British Cycling, and many other Olympic sports did the same. They know that ultimately a couple of percent can make the difference between a world record and not even making the final. This dedication to attention to detail has been documented in world class sporting organizations (Gilson, Pratt, Roberts & Weymes, 2000).

Take a moment to think about your own performance. Do you chase down all the tiny details? Do you challenge yourself to get absolutely everything as close to perfect as possible? Are there things that you'd consider were 'too small to bother about'? Many people often ask how they can get an extra 10–20 percent performance. The answer is usually pretty simple. If you find five to ten things that you can get an extra one or two percent from, you can find the 10–20 per cent you need. In the film, *Any Given Sunday*, Al Pacino describes American Football as 'a game of inches'. To be successful you need to gain every single inch that you can. The trick is to add up all the inches. He points out that the inches we need are all around us. In his words, they are in "every break of the game, every minute, every second". That's true of life. The opportunities to gain one or two percent by picking up the tiny details are all around us.

I often conduct an exercise with teams, which helps us to identify what those tiny details are. I've given it a glitzy title (because I'm a performance coach and that's what we do) – 'Creating a World Class Vision'. I first did the exercise with one of the Great Britain squads. After talking with their coaches, it became apparent that most of the coaches and most of the athletes didn't actually know what was required to become genuinely world class and compete for medals in major competitions. They had a pattern and a program that they followed. The results over the last few years clearly showed that their program produced performances that were well outside of the medals. They needed to do things differently to change their results. They needed different processes. The exercise simply asked them to identify behaviors that they would consider were *amateur, professional* and *world class*. This is what they came up with. These are the athletes' words.

Here is a slightly different example from an elite rowing crew.

Table 10.1 Creating a World Class Vision – Exercise 1

Amateur	Professional	World Class
Not giving your all	Good organization	Always highly focused
No program or plan	Good personal management	Takes on tough targets
Amateur lifestyle and diet	Consistently hits targets	Hunger and dedication
Forgets kit at times	Takes responsibility	No excuses
Goes through the motions	Trains well	Always wants to improve
Moans	Good attitude and will to win	Uses the team around them
Lack of preparation	Detailed plan and program	Always high-quality training
Takes short cuts	Records, monitors and reviews	Attends to tiny details
Lazy in training	Professional lifestyle	Always learning
Doesn't consider others	Professional diet	Never satisfied

Table 10.2 Creating a World Class Vision – Exercise 2

Amateur	Professional	World Class
Not caring in some sessions	Relishes doing sessions	Learns from everything!
Only performs when being watched	Can do it on their own	Be a role model
Falls apart under pressure	Performs when required	Questions everything
Doesn't understand the reason for sessions	Recognizes weaknesses and works on them	Self critical and improves on their own
Disorganized	Efficient in training	Does great sessions in any circumstance
Assumes everything	Communicates well with coaches	Uses negatives to improve
Doesn't question their own progression		Consistent high quality
		Vacuum for knowledge

Once we had created the tables, we also discussed how the squads felt their current practice rated in each area? Was their current practice *amateur*, *professional* or *world class*? Both squads were looking to win medals at world level, so by definition, they needed to be world class. Most of their responses suggested that they were amateur or professional, so we identified ways that they could change their practice and move towards being world class.

As you can imagine, making these kinds of changes requires a great deal of effort. It requires them to enter their discomfort zone. The squads found that as they started to change their practices, the performances started to follow. Unsurprisingly, they found that the hard work started to translate into improved results when they adopted the phrase 'train like you compete and compete like you train'. Although it seems obvious, many athletes will prepare very differently for training and competition. They will save their best preparation for competition and employ their second best for training. The result is that they don't produce their best performances regularly in training. Common sense dictates that if you don't produce higher quality performances in training, you will not produce them consistently in competition. What benefit is there in scrimping on the preparation for training sessions? The other obvious consequence is that training doesn't closely replicate the demands of competition. We don't adopt the same mindset or train ourselves to perform under true competition conditions. In a sense, they become two separate entities. This is also common sense. However, many performers are surprised that they find it difficult to transfer their 'form' in training over to competition (Taylor & Wilson, 2005).

Some of the world's greatest athletes have benefited from having an environment that constantly requires them to produce world class performances. Over the years, there have been examples where a number of the world's best athletes have been pushing each other, sometimes on a daily basis. In the 1980s, Great Britain had a group of middle-distance runners that included Seb Coe, Steve Cram, Steve Ovett and Tom McKean. This small group of athletes would regularly train and compete against each other and push each other to become ever better. They were among the very best in the world at the time. If they beat each other, the chances were that they would beat anyone else in the world. I found the same in the highly successful England Squash setup (Hartley, 2012). It also drove the success of the 2008 Olympic British cycling team. The standard of the competition in training was second to none. In order to simply make the British team, athletes would have to be capable of breaking world records. As a result, members of the team found themselves breaking records in qualifying rounds of the 2008 Olympics (Attwooll, 2008).

In the Beijing Olympic Games of 2008, Michael Phelps set a record for the number of gold medals won by a single Olympian in one Games. In his interviews, he mentioned a lesser-known U.S. swimmer called Ryan Lochte (Gonzalez, 2008). Although not as famous, Lochte has multiple Olympic medals including gold medals from both 2004 and 2008. Michael Phelps credits swimmers such as Ryan Lochte for pushing him so hard. For Phelps, being challenged to beat Lochte on a regular basis almost guarantees that he is capable of beating anyone else in the world.

We don't need to be in an Olympic program to be able to draw on that principle. There are opportunities to pitch ourselves against other great performers in our own fields. Great performers pitch themselves against other greats. They test themselves and challenge themselves. Sometimes this happens by chance. Sometimes it happens by design. Great performers will often deliberately find an opponent who can expose their weaknesses or challenge them. For example, tennis players may pitch themselves against left-handed players or players with an awkward serve because it presents them with a tough challenge. A middle-distance runner might pitch himself against fast finishers if that is one of his weaker areas. Athletes may not get their ideal challenge dropped onto their laps. Often, they go hunting for them.

Great performers make sure that their challenges always become more difficult. I often describe this as a set of hurdles that only ever get higher. There is almost no point in challenging yourself to clear a hurdle that you could manage with your eyes shut. If they are to work for us and make us better, they have to get higher. Inevitably, when we challenge ourselves with higher hurdles, we create the possibility (and probability) that we will hit some. The great performers that I've seen are not scared of hitting hurdles. One of their greatest single qualities is the ability to get up and go again. In fact, I have often noticed that the very best performers are those who have experienced the hurdles and the bumps in the road.

"The harder you work, the harder it is to surrender".

Vince Lombardi

A few years ago, I worked with two swimmers. Both were internationals in their events. They were both very professional, had a great attitude and worked exceptionally hard on their performance. In fact, they were similar in many ways. The big difference between them was their life circumstances. One had a pretty cozy life. He lived in a flat which his parents provided. He had a very comfortable life. His lifestyle was designed to allow him to focus his energies on competing and training with very few other worries. There were very few bumps in his road. By comparison, the other swimmer's journey was dominated by bumps. He didn't have the same lifestyle or luxuries and needed to take care of himself. Money was tight, life was less comfortable, and he had to make the best of it. The second swimmer often found that he had to work in imperfect conditions, find solutions and think on his feet. As you can imagine, these challenges made him stronger. He became adept at producing very high-quality performances in imperfect conditions. He was used to dealing with problems and was unfazed by the bumps in the road. The first swimmer, of course, didn't have the benefit of this experience. Whenever he encountered the bumps, it became a major issue for him. He found it difficult to perform in imperfect conditions and became flustered more easily. Although many people would advocate removing the bumps in the road, I actually think it's better to have them and use them. In many ways, removing the challenges is artificial.

No doubt, you will have witnessed exactly the same outside of sport. Whether in business or life, often those who succeed are those who had to fight to get where they are. The very process of fighting is likely to have helped them to achieve. Many great entrepreneurs have started life in what would normally be considered a 'disadvantaged' position. If you examine the life stories of many of today's business leaders, they started out with nothing (Kilpatrick, 2003; Caan, 2009; Sugar, 2010). Maybe that 'disadvantage' is in fact an advantage? Perhaps it is a disadvantage to have the trappings of a comfort zone. It is possible that the environment that many successful entrepreneurs were brought up in focused them to become successful. It presented them with the challenges and the lessons they needed in order to be successful.

It is true that great performers are incredibly focused. The great athletes that I have worked with knew exactly what they needed to do in every single session. They know that each session is valuable and that they need to extract every ounce of possible benefit from it. One day I chatted to an Olympian about his sessions for the day. He told me that in his twelve-week training cycle, today was only one of eight sessions that was specifically focused on increasing his top speed. The other sessions focused on other elements such as endurance, technique or starts. In his mind, this session was crucial. If he missed the opportunity, he only had another seven sessions to increase his top speed before his major competition at the end of the year. He also lived by the philosophy that if he became 0.1 per cent better in every session, by the end of the week he'd be almost one per cent better. By the end of the training cycle, he could be ten per cent better.

This philosophy is so simple, and yet it applies to almost every area of life. If we focus and apply ourselves to everything we do, we will start to do it a little better. If we make tiny improvements on every occasion, those improvements will add up over time. Great performances don't happen by chance. They don't happen overnight or by the click of a finger (Colvin, 2008). We don't tend to make huge leaps towards our goals, we tend to take steps. Great performers work on making a continual series of very focused small steps. They do this very deliberately, and in doing so, they take responsibility for their development and their performances.

I often see a very distinct divide between those who take responsibility for their performance and those who don't. Usually those who don't take responsibility get frustrated much more easily. Although it sounds easier to blame others, the fact is that if we fail to take responsibility, we also fail to take control (Koestenbaum & Block, 2001; Martin Fischer & Ravizza, 1998; Nesti, 2004; Hartley, 2012). In order to have control over our performance we must accept responsibility and be accountable for it (Jauncey, 2002; Hartley, 2012). Only then can we have any control. Do you remember our fencing squad back in the Introduction? Their mindset, and therefore their performances, were being controlled by everyone else and everything else because they had not taken responsibility for them. By taking responsibility, we must accept that whatever situation we find ourselves in, we have created it. This can sometimes be tough. I know this from personal experience.

I have found myself working very hard on projects which have failed to produce the results. The temptation sometimes is to look at the hard work that I've put in and conclude that the project's failure is somehow due to circumstance. It's more comfortable in the short term to put it all down to 'bad luck' or other people's failure to deliver. In reality though, the responsibility is mine. Only when I recognize this will I be able to learn from it. If I can't see the mistakes I made, I won't be able to correct them and I run the risk of doing the same thing next time and the time after that. That could get disheartening. However, if I accept responsibility, I will start looking for the reasons behind the results. Did I back a project without knowing it was definitely viable? Did I research it well enough before we started? Did I give responsibility to others without knowing that they could deliver? Did I leave some elements of the project's success to chance? The answer of course is that I made mistakes. If I recognize that I am responsible, I can start working on these issues so that I adapt my approach next time. If I fail to recognize the mistakes because I choose to blame circumstances, I will never make the changes I need to make.

The vast majority of what we need to learn comes from self-coaching (Luciani, 2004). I use this phrase deliberately. Some say that experience is the greatest teacher, but I'd tend to disagree. Experience gives you an opportunity to learn. Some take full advantage of the opportunity, others don't. The reality is that we have to be our own teachers and coaches. Ultimately, great performers often are their own coaches. Not only do they learn from their own experiences, but they also actively seek out the knowledge that they need. They are true students of their chosen field. The great athletes, coaches, and managers that I've worked with are genuine students of their sport. Great business leaders are students of business and of their industries. They have a thirst for knowledge. Their passion drives them to find out what they don't know and to understand what they don't fully understand. They constantly question and challenge the norm.

> "Question everything. Learn something. Answer nothing".
>
> Euripides (Greek playwright, c. 480–406 BC)

Many elite athletes and executives that I've worked with have a habit of questioning. They rarely take an answer or a solution at face value. Often, they will look deeper. They are keen to see whether there is a better way of doing things. They are constantly looking for improvements and refinements. As a result, they become innovators (Weisberg, 2006). This doesn't mean that they are looking to reinvent the wheel. It means that they are constantly raising the floor.

You might have read those last three words – raising the floor – and wondered if it was a misprint. Surely, I meant to say, 'raising the bar', right? Wrong. In my experience, highly successful people are focused on raising the floor. They know there is a difference between their best day, and their not-so-great day. If they were to score it on a zero-to-ten scale, they might say their best day was 9/10 but their worst was only a 5/10. Their aim is to turn that 5/10 into a 7/10 or 8/10. Their focus is to raise the floor and improve their not-so-great day. This gives them more consistency. It gives them the confidence that their worst performance is still pretty good.

This kind of thinking helps athletes become great. But, it's not limited to their sporting performance. The same thinking transcends the boundaries of sport and elevates performance in all areas of life.

Many of the Olympians that I worked with began to evolve into managers. This may seem bizarre when you consider that the majority were 'individual athletes'. Why would a swimmer, or a runner, or a gymnast need to become a good manager? The answer is quite simple. Top athletes operate like many other high performers. They surround themselves with experts (Bannatyne, 2006). Typically, a top Olympian will have coaches, a sport psychologist, medics, a physiologist, performance analyst, and a strength and conditioning coach. Each of these experts will feedback and input into the training program, preparation strategy and performance reviews. The athlete then has the task of ensuring that they manage their team, so that the team delivers. They need to become adept at drawing what they need from their team. Not only must the athlete start to coordinate their team of experts, but they must also push that team to drive performance. Great athletes encourage their teams to become critical in all areas and to keep searching for the extra one percent that will provide a performance gain. The team needs to share the athlete's vision and be able to dedicate themselves to helping the athlete achieve their goals.

If you're interested to see how elite athletes translate their performance from sport into business and life, search for *The Podium Podcast* (BWC Media, 2022). You'll find dozens of conversations, where I've asked athletes like Olympic Champion, Rebecca Adlington, and former Springboks captain, Bob Skinstad, how they use their athletic mindset to run a successful business.

This thinking can be adopted in any domain. Leaders in business, education, healthcare, and the military (to name just a few) often strive to do the same. They need to engage their teams and ensure that they get absolutely the best from each of the individuals (Jauncey, 2002). They push to ensure that their processes become better and better. While working with one particular business I was often heard saying, 'It's very good, but it's not world class yet'. Although it may sound petty anal, our aim was not to become very good. The aim of the business was to become world class in our field. In order to do that, we needed to start with very high standards and keep increasing them. We developed a *never satisfied mindset*, which is common among truly great performers, whether they be athletes, executives, surgeons, or teachers. Many of the genuinely world class athletes that I've worked with often score themselves as a 4/10 in their performances. It's ironic that many juniors will score themselves as a 9/10. Although it may seem unusual at first glance, the reason is pretty straightforward. The world class athlete is acutely aware of all of the areas they can still improve on. They have a great appreciation of the fine details and see the gap between 9.9/10 and 10/10. It is no coincidence that athletes who have this appreciation go on to become world class. Their awareness of the imperfections drives them to continually work on their game.

The almost obsessive strive for perfection can sometimes be a double-edged sword. Striving for perfection is clearly a significant factor in becoming a great performer. However, many people can almost become neurotic about their performance. Their life becomes completely dominated by it and they can lose their sense of perspective. We discussed the trapdoors that can appear when our life becomes so focused on the performance, that we lose sight of everything else (Ben-Shahar, 2009). Jonny Wilkinson (2008) described his experiences of this challenge in his book *Tackling Life: Striving for Perfection*. His accounts show that the quest for perfection can often be a pretty lonely and miserable one if your life is entirely devoted to one thing. It highlights the need for a balanced life and a broad sense of self, which we discussed in the previous chapter.

One way to achieve this is simply to focus on improving constantly, rather than perfecting. Although we need to be aware of the imperfections, we also need to focus on the improvement. Great performers in all disciplines are aware that the secret to producing a great performance is simple. The vast majority of great performers, whether they are organizations, teams or individuals, stick to a very simple rule. They do the basics exceptionally well (Gilson, Pratt, Roberts & Weymes, 2000). Great performers sometimes do extraordinary things. However, the bulk of what they do is to deliver the basics better than anyone else. If you analyze the world's best athletes and sports teams, they often don't seem to have any magical formula. They don't do anything vastly different from their opponents. Instead, they do essentially the same things, but better. The great performers might be more precise, more consistent or be able to maintain the quality of their performance for longer. They may have practiced their skills at a higher intensity, with less time or space available to them. Good coaches know that the performance we see in competition is usually lower than that on the training field, because the demands of competition are higher. Therefore, they need to raise the standard of the practice significantly, to deliver a high standard on match day. Good coaches also know that there is no point in doing anything else, until their team has absolutely mastered the basics first. And once they have absolutely mastered the basics, there is not much else to do.

I often see competitors fall apart because their opponent simply delivers the basics exceptionally well. Rackets sports, in particular illustrate it for me. I noticed an interesting pattern developing when I worked in elite Squash (Hartley, 2010, 2011). I would watch a point being played out. Often one player would play a consistent series of very accurate and precise shots. Normally these would be played into an area of the court which caused their opponents most challenges. On a squash court that tended to be the back corners. After a while, the other player would start looking for ways to break the status quo and get out of the corners. Invariably they would start playing riskier shots. The player who played consistently precise shots would then start stretching their opponent, so that the opponent's shots became weaker and provided them with opportunities to play a winner. The cumulative effect of consistently accurate shots started to take effect. After a little while, the player on the receiving end would start making forced errors when they took riskier shots; shots that were not really on. Following a couple of forced errors, the frustration would start to set in. Not long after that, we would then see the unforced errors. As you can probably imagine, unforced errors lead to further frustration and the game starts to crumble (Crust & Nesti, 2006).

The same pattern can be seen in a variety of sports fairly easily. When batters in cricket feel that they need to score runs, they will often play risky shots and therefore stand a much greater chance of getting themselves out. Equally, if bowlers feel that they desperately need a wicket, they may bowl more erratically and therefore stand more chance of giving away runs. The same decisions can be seen throughout sports. Quarter backs in the NFL throw more interceptions when they are continually denied time and space, or when they need yards to make a first down. Often it takes a great deal of resolve to avoid forcing plays that aren't there. When the game starts to go against them, I often see teams throw the game plan out of the window and start playing off the cuff.

To me, one element of mental toughness is composure – the ability to make great decisions and execute really well, whatever happens (Hartley, 2018). It means being able to stick to the game plan and stay focused on doing the simple things well, consistently. This principle is recognized outside of sport. Mark Douglas applies the same mindset to trading on the stock exchange (Douglas, 2000). So often, individuals and teams forget the game plan completely when they are asked some serious questions. Often, they don't have enough knowledge of the game plan or enough confidence in it. Many people ask me why it is that champion teams can always seem to nick a win at the last minute. Why is it that they always win by a narrow margin rather than lose? Perhaps they have absolute faith in their game plan and their ability to execute it? As a result, they keep delivering their processes until the very last minute. Maybe their opposition starts to crumble and waver in the face of this, and consequently abandons their game plan at the last minute? It is true that sometimes tactics need changing. However, a change of tactics should be a part of the overall game plan. The plan should be something that has been practiced, rehearsed and stress-tested so that it is second nature.

In 2006, Great Britain's Chris Cook won the 100m breaststroke final at the Commonwealth Games. He turned fifth at the halfway point. As he turned, he knew that he'd delivered his first 50m according to his game plan. He didn't worry. He didn't change his game plan. Chris knew that he had a very specific plan, which was designed for him and drew on his individual strengths. It was his. In fact, it probably would not have suited anyone else in the race. Chris was so confident in his plan that he simply kept delivering it until he hit the wall to finish. As a result, he took home the gold medal.

One of the reasons that Chris found it so easy to stick to the plan is that he knew it was his. It was very personal to him. It was authentic. We hadn't adapted it from someone else's game plan or copied it. The race plan was created by Chris and for Chris. We could only do this because Chris knew himself. He knew himself and could therefore be himself. He had confidence in himself as a person and an athlete. This confidence allowed him to be himself and deliver his performance. In my experience, this is one of the strongest characteristics of a world class performer. It allows them to keep things really simple and stick to their very simple job. Authenticity goes hand in hand with true success. Only when we know ourselves, accept ourselves and allow ourselves to be authentic, can we truly deliver great performances (Seligman, 2005; Orlick, 1998; Csikszentmihalyi, 1990; Frankl, 1959/1984).

In summary …

- Great performers are often not the most naturally gifted.
- Often the great performers are those who go the extra mile and get the tiny details right.
- Continually test yourself and push to become better. Look for higher hurdles and tougher challenges.
- When you take responsibility, you take control.
- Be your self.

References

Attwooll, J. (2008) 'Great Britain break world record in the team sprint cycling: Team GB have got their track cycling campaign in Beijng off to a flying start by breaking the world record in the team sprint qualification rounds'. *Daily Telegraph.* 15th August 2008. Online. Available www.telegraph.co.uk/sport/othersports/olympics/2562987/Britain-breaks-world-record-in-the-Team-Sprint-cycling-Beijing-Olympics-2008.html (accessed 15th December 2010).

Bannatyne, D. (2006) *Anyone Can Do It: My Story,* London: Orion.

Ben-Shahar, T. (2009) *The Pursuit of Perfect: How to Stop Chasing Perfection and Start Living a Richer, Happier Life,* New York: McGraw Hill Professional.

BWC Media (2022) *The Podium Podcast.* Online. Available https://linktr.ee/bwcmedia (accessed 30th November 2022).

Caan, J. (2009) *The Real Deal: My Story from Brick Lane to Dragon's Den,* London: Virgin.

Colvin, G. (2008) *Talent is Overrated: What Really Separates World Class Performers from Everybody Else,* New York: Portfolio.

Crust, L. and Nesti, M.S. (2006) 'A review of psychological momentum in sports: Why qualitative research is needed', *Athletic Insights,* 8(1), 1–15.

Csikszentmihalyi, M. (1990). *Flow: The Psychology of Optimal Experience,* New York: Harper and Row.

Douglas, M. (2000) *The Disciplined Trader: Developing Winning Attitudes,* New Jersey: Prentice Hall.

Dweck, C.S. (2007) *Mindset: The New Psychology of Success,* New York: Ballantine Books.

Farrow, D., Baker, J. and MacMahon, C. (2007) *Developing Sport Expertise: Researchers and Coaches Put Theory into Practice,* London: Routledge.

Frankl, V. E. (1959/1984). *Man's Search for Meaning,* New York: Touchstone.

Gilson, C., Pratt, M., Roberts, K. and Weymes, E. (2000) *Peak Performance: Business Lessons from the World's Top Sports Organisations*, New York: Harper Collins Business.

Gladwell, M. (2008) *Outliers: The Story of Success*, London: Little, Brown & Co.

Gonzalez, J. (2008) '0.27 seconds: All that separates Michael Phelps and Ryan Lochte', *Men's Journal*, 16th July 2008.

Hartley, S.R. (2010) 'Momentum shifts in sport: Value the psychology behind them', *Podium Sports Journal*, December 2010. Available online. www.podiumsportsjournal.com/2010/12/22/momentum-shifts-in-sports-value-the-psychology-behind-them/> (accessed 4th April 2011).

Hartley, S.R. (2011) 'Maintaining momentum', *Squash Player*, 39(2), 28–29.

Hartley, S.R. (2012) *How to Shine; Insights Into Unlocking Your Potential From Proven Winners*, Chichester: Capstone.

Hartley, S.R. (2018) *Master Mental Toughness*, Leeds: Be World Class.

Jauncey, P. (2002) *Managing Yourself and Others*, Brisbane: CopyRight Publishing.

Kilpatrick, A. (2003) *Of Permanent Value: The Story of Warren Buffett*, New York: APKE.

Koestenbaum, P. and Block, P. (2001) *Freedom and Accountability at Work: Applying Philosophic Insight to the Real World*, New York: Jossey Bass.

Luciani, J.J. (2004) *The Power of Self-Coaching: The 5 Essential Steps to Creating the Life You Want*, New York: Wiley.

Martin Fischer, J. and Ravizza, M. (1998) *Responsibility and Control: A Theory of Moral Responsibility*, Cambridge: Cambridge University Press.

Nesti, M.S. (2004) *Existential Psychology and Sport: Theory and Application*, Oxford: Routledge.

Orlick, T. (1998) *Embracing Your Potential*, Champaign, IL: Human Kinetics.

Seligman, M.E.P. (2005) *Authentic Happiness: Using the New Positive Psychology to Realize Your Potential for Lasting Fulfillment*, New York: Free Press.

Starkes, J.L. and Ericsson, K.A. (2003) *Expert Performance in Sports: Advances in Research on Sport Expertise*, Champaign, IL: Human Kinetics.

Sugar, A. (2010) *What You See is What You Get: My Autobiography*, London: Macmillan.

Taylor, J. & Wilson, G.S. (2005) *Applying Sport Psychology: Four Perspectives*, Champaign, IL: Human Kinetics.

Weisberg, R. (2006) *Creativity: Understanding Innovation in Problem Solving, Science, Invention, and the Arts*, New York: Wiley.

Wilkinson, J. (2008) *Tackling Life: Striving for Perfection*, London: Headline.

Coaching Others to Achieve Peak Performances

11

I left school with an A grade in GCSE mathematics, so I confidently packed my bags and went off to college to study it at A Level. A couple of weeks into the course, I found that maths was, all of a sudden, much more difficult. My fellow classmates, who had also achieved decent grades at GCSE, also struggled.

How is it possible to take a group of 'capable' mathematics students, and erode their performance so quickly?

This is what happened …

Our lecturer would set us a series of tasks (normally from the trusty text-book) and we would have a go at them. Inevitably our answers were incorrect, so our lecturer would show us what we'd done wrong and set us another series of exercises to try. We repeated this pattern time after time … for two whole years. I honestly felt no wiser going into the exam room at the end of two years, than I did on day one. Consequently, I was one of the 70 percent of my class that came out with an *ungraded* mark (a fail) at the end of my course. Some of the class did reach the heady heights of an E or a D grade, but the vast majority of us didn't even get that far.

At the time, the experience didn't strike me as being very useful. I felt like I'd wasted two years of my life on the subject. However, a few years later, I started to see the same patterns again in a different situation. This time I saw it in a professional football dressing room. The manager would sit the players down at half time and explain to them where they were going wrong. He'd then send them out for the second half and was always amazed that they didn't simply go out and put things right. I used to see the constant frustration in the manager, which reminded me of my maths lecturer. Both the manager and my lecturer had made the same mistake. They assumed that pointing out the errors would automatically lead to the solution. The fact is, as human

DOI: 10.4324/9781003181491-12

beings, we often need more than that. Understanding where we went wrong is fine but is not enough. We also need to know how we should be performing, and we need to be able to practice it. Practicing is absolutely crucial if we're going to change our performance.

Often the manager would ask the team to change their tactics or their formation on the field to counter what the opposition was doing. The problem was, our players hadn't practiced doing that. They'd never played in the formation before or practiced the new tactics. It was not simply a case of switching to something they knew and were confident in. Therefore, they tried it initially, found that it didn't work very well, so they reverted to what they did know. As the manager moaned at them for making the same mistakes time after time, the players' confidence started to drain away. The players (just like our maths class) didn't know what to do or how to do it.

It's not just football managers (or maths lecturers) that fall into this pattern. I'm sure you will have seen it, been on the receiving end of it, or maybe even fallen into it yourself at some point. So, what's the alternative? How do we turn around performances, undo negative spirals, start positive spirals and change our results?

I will try to explain this using a real-life example of a professional football team in the U.K. We'll take it step by step and I'll show you the process we used to turn around the performance. At the start of the process the team was losing, the strikers had become shot-shy, confidence was ebbing away, and the squad had started to argue, blame each other and moan. Morale was pretty low. So where did we start?

It might sound obvious, but we need to start at the beginning. We started from zero.

Step one is to clarify and simplify. First, we need to ensure that everyone understands their job in the simplest possible terms. If we're working in a team, we need to know the job of the team. What is its reason to exist? What does it need to do to be successful and achieve its targets?

In our football team, it was simple. Let's get right back to basics. We're trying to score more goals than the opposition. That means that we need to score more and concede less. Everyone in the team has a role to play in those two jobs. Every player needs to know their role in simple clear terms (Bray & Brawley, 2002a, 2002b). When we started the exercise with the coaching staff, I asked what each player's role was in those jobs. Their answers were a little woolly to start with. The fact is that if the coaching staff weren't clear, how would the players be clear? After a little work, we started to clarify each and every person's role and what we needed from them.

Now that we know the job, and we have clarified the roles for each person, we can set about putting step two into place and start building confidence.

One of the fundamental strategies to build confidence is to start with the things people can do well. Therefore, as part of this exercise I was keen to know how we could help the players by making their jobs as easy as possible.

At the football club, we spent a long time looking through the video footage of the matches. The club already had a great deal of performance analysis data and clips of the players that were catalogued. This allowed us to pick out all the instances where the players performed well, and all of those in which the players struggled. Once we had these, we looked for patterns. One of the center forwards struggled in certain positions on the field. He also struggled when he was asked to receive certain types of passes. When we analyzed the overall footage, we found that he was forced to play to his weaknesses for the majority of the game. However, there were instances where he looked extremely comfortable, effective, and dangerous. Again, there were patterns. He was most effective in specific areas of the field and when he could receive short, fast, accurate passes. So, we needed to change way the team played slightly to help this player become more effective.

Once we had the information on one player, we could also find out how the others played at their best. We could see when they were most comfortable and most effective. We could also see where they struggled and when their weaknesses were being exposed. Gradually we built up a picture of the squad and started to form a game plan which drew on their strengths. We then set about putting this into practice on the training field. Gradually, we increased the intensity and the demands so that our practice became like competition. This builds up so that, eventually, the challenges we set in practice surpassed the demands of competition.

Even though we need to start building confidence by focusing on the things our people can do, we also need to progress by working on those things they are not so good at. There will be weaknesses that people need to work hard on, so that they can become confident in those areas.

We put this into action in the football club by structuring each player's practice so that they gradually become more and more confident in the areas they previously struggled with. Obviously, this doesn't happen overnight. Not only do they need to practice, but they need to test themselves in competitive situations. The players and coaches know that learning requires time and mistakes, so as much of this as possible is done on the training field rather than on match day. Once they're comfortable and confident, they'll start to bring more into competitive games. Realistically, we know that it won't be perfect and that there will always be mistakes and learning at this stage.

If we have made solid progress with the first few steps, we should have started the positive spiral. In order to build confidence, we will need to ensure that we're evaluating honestly and objectively. We need to focus on the performance and the process, not the results. Normally there is a delay between the performance improvement and the corresponding change in results.

At the football club, we were conscious that each player had a very clear job and that they should be evaluated against that job. The coaching staff were very careful to make sure that their feedback was evaluative (rather than judgmental), honest, objective and focused on the delivery of that player's job. There was no room for blame or excuses. Everyone was charged with taking responsibility for their role and delivering it to the best of their ability. Win, lose or draw, we needed to stick to this process.

This same process can be used in larger organizations. I have recently been working with businesses, helping them to increase their performance. We start by simplifying and clarifying. I normally use the *Two Lengths of the Pool* analogy that we discussed in Chapter 3 (Hartley, 2013). With an organization, the first stage is to understand the job of the organization in the simplest possible terms. This normally takes time. I am always amazed at the variety of responses I get from board members of the same company when I ask them to describe the organization's job.

When we know the job of the organization, we can then start to define the jobs for each group, team, and department within the business. As we do this, we must ensure that the job for every team is aligned with the overall *Two Lengths of the Pool* for the organization. Each team needs to contribute fully to the organization. We need to know that if each team delivers its job, the organization will be successful in its job.

This exercise is then cascaded down through the organization so that each person knows their own job in the simplest possible terms (Donnelly & Ivancevich, 1975). Everyone should know their own job and see how it contributes to their team and ultimately to the organization. This alignment brings clarity.

Once we have those foundations in place, we will be able to add newer, greater and more demanding challenges. We can start venturing into the discomfort zone. Gradually, we can ask our people to start pushing their boundaries. We can start picking up on the fine details. We can start looking for better delivery and more consistency in more demanding situations. We can raise the targets and the standards.

This is a process that has been used to good effect in some Olympic sports. A number of Olympic Performance Directors in the U.K. took the bold step of setting a new standard for athletes to achieve (Harris, 2009). One Performance Director made it clear that there was no point in having athletes on the program who didn't have genuine medal winning prospects. Therefore, to get on the program and receive any funding, every athlete needed to be producing world class times in their events. The bar was set. Let's imagine the process. Initially, the athletes need to get into the top 12 in the world. It is a tough challenge but many of them work hard and achieve it. They take a sigh of relief. They are in the program and have secured their funding. Then the bar rises. Now the athletes need to be in the top 10, so they push themselves again. As before, many make it. Phew! I'm sure you're ahead of me already. That's right, once they make top 10 the bar rises again to top eight, and finally top six.

So, how did the coaches help those athletes continually make the improvements necessary to get over that rising bar? The formula is pretty straightforward. As a coach you need to set a *plan, do and review* process into play. It's embarrassingly simple. We outlined the basic principles in Chapter 5.

I often start by asking people to identify the most important elements of their performance. I tend to limit this to the most significant five elements – those which have the biggest impact on their performance. When the athlete gets these five things right, a peak performance is almost guaranteed. In Chapter 3, we outlined the *Five Keys* (Hartley, 2013). Those would be a perfect starting point. To be honest, this part of the exercise alone is worth its weight in gold. It helps the athlete really understand what drives their performance and what makes a difference to them.

Once we have these elements, I ask the athlete to start rating themselves using a zero-to-ten scale. A score of ten means 'perfect, flawless, every single time'. When I conduct this exercise with athletes or executives, I often challenge, and stress-test the scores to make sure that they are justified. This also helps me to understand the athlete's experience in more detail. For example, if a long jumper rated his approach to the board as a 6/10, it's useful to know why. It might be because he feels that the run up gets choppy towards the end, or that the stride pattern needs changing. Understanding the reason of course helps us to make improvements to that element.

Now that we have a score for each element, we can start to set targets and strategies to improve each area. Very simply, I ask the athlete and their coach how they can close the gap between their current level of performance and their target level. We talk through their strategies and the training plan. At this stage, I also ask the athlete to describe the differences between their current level and their target. For example, if they are a 6/10 today and they have a target to get to 8/10 in six weeks, we need to know what an 8/10 will look like. How will we know when we get there? What will we see, hear, or feel that is different? How will the athlete think, act, and talk when they are an 8/10? We need to create a meaning behind the number. I also tend to chat to the athlete about the difference those two points will make to their performance. We discuss the benefits of getting this element to 8/10 and what impact it is likely to have in their performance. This helps the athlete really start to understand the reasons to work on this element and the importance of making the changes.

This process starts to give us a structure for the athlete's development and a mechanism to review progress. Because it is so simple and yet so effective, I have used it with a huge variety of performers, from show jumpers to sales executives. It is an incredibly versatile tool and I suspect it can be used to help increase human performance in any field.

But, it's only a plan.

Experience has taught me that a plan, on its own, achieves very little. If we're to employ a 'Plan – Do – Review' cycle, we need to put the plan into action. We need to 'Do' what's in the plan. Although it sounds blindingly obvious, there's often a huge gap between knowing what to do, and actually doing it.

So, how do we bridge the gap between 'knowing' and 'doing'?

This is the focus of our final chapter.

In summary…

- Start with clarity and simplicity.
- Build on what you can do, play to your strengths and work on your weaknesses.
- Build your confidence through practice, performance and reviews.
- Be constantly aware of how you can improve.
- Plan – Do – Review.

References

Bray, S.R. and Brawley, L.R. (2002a) 'Role efficacy, role clarity and role performance effectiveness', *Small Group Research*, 33(2), 233–253.

Bray, S.R. and Brawley, L.R. (2002b) 'Efficacy for independent role functions: Evidence from the sport domain, *Small Group Research*, 33(6), 644–666.

Donnelly, J.H. and Ivancevich, J.M. (1975) 'Role clarity and the salesman', *Journal of Marketing*, 39(1), 71–74.

Harris, N. (2009) 'In the pool: Team GB can make a bigger splash in 2012', *The Independent*, 18th March 2009.

Hartley, S.R. (2013) *Two Lengths of the Pool: Sometimes the Simplest Ideas Have the Greatest Impact*, Leeds: Be World Class.

The Power of Character 12 and Identity

Over the years, I've had a lot of conversations with sales executives about goals. They've all got goals and targets which they want to hit. They've also got a plan. They know exactly how many sales calls they need to make, and how many meetings they need to have.

And yet, they don't put the plan into action and therefore don't hit their goals.

It's not just sales goals of course. People have health and fitness goals – maybe to lose weight or get their blood sugar levels down. They know what to do. The strategy is pretty simple – eat and drink healthy stuff, cut out the junk, exercise, get some fresh air and a decent amount of sleep. It's not rocket science. But, despite knowing what to do, a lot of people struggle to do it.

So, what's the gap between 'knowing' and 'doing'?

I often explain it by saying that the gap between knowing and doing is *being*.

To do the stuff we know we should do; we need to *be* different.

We might need to become more tenacious (so that we keep going and don't quit as easily), or more resilient (so that we bounce back from setbacks, rather than being floored by them), or more consistent … or patient … or courageous. In fact, we might need to develop a few different characteristics – importantly; tenacity, resilience, courage, consistency and patience are all desirable characteristics. They are elements of our character (Hartley, 2015, 2018).

So far, through the course of this book, we have concentrated on aspects of our mindset that I refer to as our 'mental game' – i.e., focus, confidence, motivation etc. I see the 'mental game' as our ability to manage the moment-by-moment flow of thoughts and feelings. Over the years, I've noticed that whenever the word 'mindset' is used, it tends to refer to this process. For example, how to change a negative thought into a positive one, when it appears in our minds, or how to change our emotional state if we feel anxious.

DOI: 10.4324/9781003181491-13

But where do these thoughts and feelings flow from?

My experiences of working in performance psychology for almost 30 years have taught me that the 'spring' from which our thoughts and feelings flow is a combination of character and identity. In my view, character and identity are the foundation of 'mindset'.

What do I mean by the words 'character' and 'identity'?

The American Psychological Association defines character as, "the totality of an individual's attributes and personality traits, particularly his or her characteristic moral, social, and religious attitude". (American Psychological Association, 2022). Personality is often described as the mental attributes that make us distinctive. Importantly, character is not just the personality traits. It's not just the mental attributes. Character has a deeper dimension – a moral dimension. Honesty is a characteristic, as is integrity and sincerity. Kindness and generosity are also characteristics.

I describe my character as, "The outward expression of who I am. It's the way I live personal qualities, my values, my beliefs, and my philosophy". Importantly, it's not just having the values and the beliefs. I could value honesty, but I'm only an honest person if I live that value.

Identity often goes hand in hand with character. Our identity is often defined as our "sense of self" (American Psychological Association, 2022). It's the way we see ourselves and what we believe about ourselves. Elements of our psyche, such as self-belief and self-worth are functions of our identity.

Whenever I ask elite coaches to describe 'the stuff of champions', they tell me about character and identity – dedication, self-discipline, persistence and self-belief. It's the same whenever I ask leaders to describe the 'stuff' they need in their people. Researcher, Paul Stoltz, and his team surveyed 10,000 employers across the United States. They asked employers who they'd prefer to hire:

Option A – the person with the best CV (skills, qualifications, experience etc.), or

Option B – the person with the right attitude and character.

Incredibly, 98 percent of those surveyed said, "Option B" (Stoltz, 2015).

So, how do we shape our character and sculpt our identity?

Perhaps the first thing to realize is that character and identity are not fixed and they're not purely a function of genetics. While many people still ask whether they are a product of 'nature or nurture', research over the past couple of decades consistently shows that it's both. The important question seems to be, how much is 'nature' and how much is 'nurture'? More specifically, how much is influenced by our DNA, and how much is influenced by how we respond to our environment and life experiences? It's a question that has fascinated researchers such as Paul Avery. When comparing biological and fraternal twins, he and his team found that genetic factors account for up to 31 percent (Arvey, et al., 2006; Arvey, et al., 2007). Therefore, the way we respond to our environment and life experiences has a far larger impact.

Our own experience probably confirms this. Are you the same person you were at 15 years of age? Did you have exactly the same characteristics then as you do now? Do you see yourself the same way now as you did then? Or, has your character and identity evolved?

A quick reflection on our own life shows that our character and identity are constantly evolving. Whether we are deliberate and intentional about *how* they evolve is another matter entirely. I suspect that most people don't consciously drive this evolution. As a result, they don't become the person they want to be. Instead, they end up becoming the person they are without really understanding how. However, we can start to develop both the characteristics we want and sculpt the way we see ourselves *if* we understand the mechanics.

As Johann Wolfgang von Goethe said, "Character is formed in the stormy billows of the world". His insight tells us that character is developed through challenge. As I've also learned, it's the choices we make when we hit those challenges that really shapes our character (Hartley, 2015). As an example, courage is not the absence of fear. Instead, it's the ability to step towards those things we're afraid of. Whenever we encounter something scary, we have a choice. Do we choose to approach it, or retreat? If we choose to step towards it, we become more courageous. In fact, every choice we make shapes our character. If we continually approach the things that scare us, we become ever more courageous.

Tenacity is our ability to keep going, especially when things get tough or painful. What do we choose to do when we hit 'the quit point' – that moment when you're tempted to throw in the towel? The choice you make in that moment shapes your tenacity.

This dynamic exists around all our characteristics. Do we choose to lie or be honest? Of course, some of the challenges are tougher than others. There are times when being completely honest is more uncomfortable. What if we're embarrassed by the truth, or ashamed of it? If we choose honesty, especially when it's more difficult, we become a more honest person.

We encounter these choices every day. Life presents them to us as a natural part of living. However, we don't have to wait for the challenges to cross our path. If we want to deliberately develop certain characteristics, we can challenge ourselves. In 2018, I constructed a challenge to develop consistency. I knew that I wasn't a particularly consistent person. I'd start something but would often tail off after a while if I lost the momentum, or my attention was drawn by a 'shiny new project'. So, I challenged myself to run 1000 miles in the year and do 1000 push-ups every month for the year. The challenge demanded that I become consistent. I'd often wake up and think, 'Do I really want to do my push-ups this morning?' There were occasions when I considered not going for a run (despite having it in my calendar), because I was tired, or because it was freezing cold and dark outside. The choices I made in these moments shaped my consistency.

If you think of these characteristics as a muscle, I began flexing this muscle every day and built the strength. As a result, I not only completed my challenge, but developed the characteristic of consistency that I can now use in all areas of my life.

If you're interested, I captured a little video and posted it on our YouTube Channel – https://youtu.be/2e3BdaUCcc8.

Knowing that our character is the totality of our characteristics, it's the culmination of these choices that ultimately shapes our character (Hartley, 2022).

In a very similar vein, our identity is the culmination of all the beliefs we've formed about ourselves. If character is built on the choices we make, identity is built on the beliefs we form. And, if we understand that belief and confidence operate in a very similar way, we can also see how to take control over how we construct these beliefs.

Back in Chapter 4, we highlighted the importance of controlling our confidence by controlling how we interact with the evidence. Sculpting our identity uses very similar principles. To build accurate and healthy beliefs, we need to engage with the evidence actively and consciously. Most people don't!

Here's an example of how unhealthy and inaccurate beliefs could be built.

A couple of years ago I had a conversation with my wife. She was making dinner for our daughters and said, "I always cook pasta for the girls". In essence, she was criticizing herself for not giving them a varied enough diet. So, I asked, "Just for interest, when was the last time you cooked pasta for them?". She looked a little quizzical and replied, "I don't know … a week ago … maybe a couple of weeks ago". Then I asked, "So, do you *always* cook pasta for the girls?"

The truth is, she probably made a pasta dish every 10 days or so. However, left unchecked, that embryonic belief will start to solidify. The next time my wife cooked pasta (even if that was two weeks later), she'd probably say to herself, 'You see … You're doing it again. You always cook pasta'.

We tend to form beliefs by looking for evidence that confirms what we already believe (Gray, 2010). Of course, this means that faulty beliefs, founded on unsound or inaccurate evidence, can become very strong. Even if only one percent of the evidence supports what we believe, that's the part we'll look for and see. It's a self-perpetuating phenomenon, like a snowball rolling down a hill. I often describe it by saying that whenever we confirm what we already believe, we wrap that belief in another layer of concrete.

Professor Todd Kashdan describes the way we develop these beliefs about ourselves using the analogy of balls and buckets (Kashdan, 2009; Kashdan & Savostyanova, 2011). He uses the example of social confidence and social anxiety.

Imagine you walk into a room full of people you don't know. You have a couple of options. You could go up to someone and start a conversation. Or, you could look around, see that no one is coming to talk to you and start checking messages on your phone. If you choose to strike up a conversation with someone, you place a ball into the 'social confidence' bucket. If you choose to check your phone, you place the ball in the 'social anxiety' bucket. Then, as you walk away from that experience, you ask yourself whether you're a socially confident person or a socially anxious one. And, with the evidence you have, you might conclude you're socially anxious.

What happens when you next walk into a room of people you don't know? The chances are, you'll probably walk in already thinking you're a socially anxious person. And, if you've given yourself that label, how are you likely to act? Will you approach people and start a conversation, or are you more likely to have a quick look around and then check your phone? If you do the latter, a second ball lands in the social anxiety bucket.

Each time we go through this process, we reinforce what we already believe about ourselves.

Your Identity

Figure 12.1 The Identity Cycle.

Of course, if we start to believe we're a socially anxious person, we start to act like one. We send out messages (often non-verbal), that tell everyone else we're not comfortable talking to people. Therefore, they're less likely to seek us out. And so, the cycle perpetuates.

As Todd Kashdan explains, after a while we become so convinced that we're socially anxious (so ingrained into the habit of placing the ball into that particular bucket), we forget the 'social confidence' bucket exists. We forget that we have a choice. We end up concluding that, 'I'm just a socially anxious person. It's just who I am'. And, perhaps most importantly, we forget that it's who we have become!

We have the ability to shape our character, through the choices we make.

We have the ability to sculpt our identity, through the beliefs we form.

Once we embrace this, we lay the foundations for a mindset that can deliver our peak performance, every time.

In summary …

- The gap between knowing and doing, is *being*.
- Elite coaches and leaders know that character and identity are 'the stuff of champions'.
- We develop our character through the choices we make when we hit the challenges.
- We develop our identity through the beliefs we form about ourselves.
- As we embrace this, we can deliberately and intentionally develop the characteristics and identity that will drive our performance and success.

References

American Psychological Association (2022) *APA Dictionary of Psychology*, online. Available https://dictionary.apa.org/ (accessed 18th January 2023).

Arvey, R.D., Rotundo, M., Johnson, W., Zhang, Z. and McGue (2006) 'The determinants of leadership role occupancy: Genetic and personality factors'. *Leadership Quarterly*, 17, 1–20.

Arvey, R.D., Zhang, Z., Avolio, B. and Krueger, R.F. (2007) 'Development and genetic determinants of leadership role occupancy among women'. *Journal of Applied Psychology*, 92, 693–706.

Gray, P.O. (2010) *Psychology*. New York: Worth Publishers.

Hartley, S.R. (2015) *How to Develop Character*, Leeds: Be World Class.

Hartley, S.R. (2018) *Master Mental Toughness*, Leeds: Be World Class.

Hartley, S.R. (2022) *Silence Your Demons*, Leeds: Be World Class.

Kashdan. T. (2009) 'Can We Change Our Personality?', Huffington Post, 17th October 2009.

Kashdan, T. and Savostyanova, A.A. (2011) 'Capturing the biases of socially anxious people by addressing partner effects and situational parameters', *Behavioral Therapy*, 42(2), 211–223.

Stoltz, P. (2015) *GRIT: The New Science of What it Takes to Persevere, Flourish and Succeed*. San Luis Obispo, CA: Climb Strong Press.

Theoretical Background and Further Reading

The purpose of this book is to provide very tangible and practical guidance on how to achieve peak performances consistently. It draws on my experiences as a practicing sport psychology consultant and performance coach working with athletes, executives, sports teams, corporations, charities and education. Therefore, the methods and approaches contained in this book are grounded in real-world experience and real life. There is a great deal of research and theoretical background which underpins the work. However, the approaches were not born out of the theory. In short, this book does not show how theory has been applied, but rather how real-world practice is underpinned by the theory. It would be true to say that I have been influenced, guided, and even inspired by some of the literature that is cited here. However, there is no single theoretical approach or paradigm. My approach to practice is influenced by a range of theories and methods. Some of these have reasonably obvious links and overlap with each other. Most are complementary. However, some may actually appear to conflict with each other theoretically.

I also take the view that theories are simply ways of trying to conceptualize the world and make sense of it. As humans, we love to find patterns and attach rules to phenomena. That's what science does. However, research and the theoretical perspectives that are generated from it, are often the subject of interpretation. They are conceived by people, who bring their experiences, views and perspectives with them. Often researchers and academics start to favor certain approaches and theoretical models over others. As a result, academic literature contains many discussions about the merits of one theory over another. I have no interest in engaging in the academic debates, or to critically appraise the merits of the various theories or research studies.

DOI: 10.4324/9781003181491-14

From a personal perspective, as a student I was influenced by a lecturer who had an appreciation of existential approaches. I found that existential methods resonated with me. I was also taught to take a broad view of the discipline of psychology, and to recognize the range of paradigms and approaches. This experience helped me to understand that sport psychology is dominated by cognitive-behavioral approaches. While I'm not against this approach per se, I would argue that focusing on one approach alone provides quite a narrow and limited view.

The purpose of this book is to help you to enhance your performance and that of others. I believe that there are some very valuable approaches that lie beyond the boundaries of mainstream, cognitive-behavioral, sport psychology. Therefore, much of the theoretical underpinning here comes from approaches such as existentialism, humanistic psychology, positive psychology, Jungian psychology, neuroscience, coaching, personal development, education, business, management, philosophy and even spirituality. The bibliography includes some very notable academics, plus authors who write almost purely from their experience. The references that are used within this book are there to signpost you to further reading, should you wish to delve deeper. There are some targeted pieces of research in specific areas, plus some background texts on the underpinning theories, as well as some practical literature that may help you to apply some of the methods yourself. The aim of this chapter is not to debate these. It is simply to give you a little more background, and outline some of these resources in a little more detail. There are some central themes, that run throughout the book and underpin most of the approaches used. I will discuss these themes first. However, there are some topic-specific approaches that also have theoretical underpinning and deserve attention.

Central Themes

The central themes revolve around several fundamental principles.

First, we have ultimate control over our performance because we have ultimate control over how we think and how we feel.

This central principle is supported by approaches in both philosophy and psychology. Concepts such as *free will*, *choice* and *responsibility* are at the heart of existentialism. Existentialism is based on the notion that, as human beings, we have both the freedom and responsibility to live a fulfilling life. As humans, we have both the power and responsibility to choose how we experience the world. In fact, existentialists would argue that freedom and responsibility are inseparable, and bound together because we have choice. We may not choose our circumstances, but ultimately our choices govern our lived experience. These principles are central to the works of authors such as Rollo May (1953), Ilman Dilman (1999), John Martin Fischer and Martin Ravizza (1998), Ronald Valle and Steen Halling (1989) and Peter Koestenbaum (2001). Ernesto Spinelli (1996) outlines existential approaches to psychology. Rollo May, who was President at Saybrook Graduate School in San Francisco, writes from an existential psychological perspective, but has also been influenced by humanistic and Freudian approaches. Ilman Dilman is professor Emeritus of Philosophy at the University of Wales, and writes on philosophical psychology and existentialism. By contrast, Peter Koestenbaum, held a professorship in Philosophy at San Jose State University for over 30 years before focusing on applying his knowledge to leadership development. Charles Manz (2000, 2002), Professor of Leadership at University of Massachusetts, also applies philosophy to business consultancy and management. Therefore, both Koestenbaum and Manz offer a more applied perspective on existential approaches. William Glasser (1999), M.D, is a psychiatrist who presents Choice Theory. Although Glasser's theory comes from a cognitive-behavioral background, it also suggests that the only person whose behavior we can control is our own; other people control themselves. Glasser also draws on many of Abram Maslow's (1998) humanistic principles.

The existential views on freedom, responsibility and choice are extended through the concept of *authenticity*. This book provides numerous illustrations of the need to be ourselves in order to perform at our peak. For example, if we are worried about what other people think of us, or how we might be judged, we often fail to perform at our peak.

Existentialists would also argue that authenticity, being yourself, is crucial if we are to lead a fulfilled life. This principle is central to the work of Rollo May, and many other existential writers. However, it is not restricted to existentialists. A contemporary and critical perspective is taken by Andrew Potter (2010), who gained a PhD in philosophy from the University of Toronto before becoming a journalist and author. His book examines why our search for authenticity in the modern world often, ironically, leads us to follow the next great 'fad'. Martin Seligman (2005), a professor of psychology at the University of Pennsylvania and former president of the American Psychological Association (APA), approaches the subject of authenticity from the perspective of positive psychology.

In order to be our self, we need to know our self.

The principle of authenticity is closely aligned with self-knowledge. Anthony Hatzomoysis (2010) is a professor of philosophy at the University of Athens. His book recognizes that self-knowledge has always been a central topic of philosophical inquiry, and he provides critical insight into the complexities of knowing one's self. That point alone is worth considering. It is hard to think of a major philosopher, from ancient times to the present, who refrained from pronouncing on the nature and the importance of self-knowledge. Self-knowledge has been a cornerstone of philosophy for centuries. Therefore, it must surely have significant importance to humanity. Maybe, it is something that we ought to take seriously as a foundation of performance. John Corlett (1996) argues that self-knowledge be recognized and embraced by sport psychology. Mark Nesti (2004) goes on to argue that free will, responsibility, choice, authenticity and self-knowledge, are all central to sport psychology theory and practice. His book provides a critical appraisal of existential approaches within sport psychology and illustrates how they have been successfully applied within elite sport settings such as Premier League football.

In order to be authentic, we often have to transcend our ego.

Our ego creates a facade. It attempts to present an image of us to the world, in the hope that the world will see us as the person we'd like to be. The work of Roy Baumeister (1993), a professor in social psychology at Florida State University, shows how threat to the ego, self-consciousness and self-presentation motivations negatively impacts on performance. His work also shows the impact that expectations have in the creation of 'pressure'.

These concepts are also outlined by authors such as Abraham Tesser (2005), professor of psychology at the University of Georgia. He developed the self-evaluation maintenance model and described, from a social psychologist's perspective, how we build, defend and regulate our notions of self. Thomas Metzinger (2010) is an academic German philosopher whose book presents a view of the ego from both philosophy and neuroscience. He explains how the ego provides us with a view of our self, which builds on his work on the study of consciousness.

Daniel Lapsley and Clark Power, from Notre Dame University (1988) provide a perspective on ego, self and identity from educational and developmental psychology. Andrew Sparkes (1998), professor of sport and pedagogy at Liverpool John Moores University and Rebecca Symes (2010), a practicing chartered sport psychologist, look at identity in an athletic context.

Of course, a journey into these realms inevitably leads to debates on the nature and existence of the self, consciousness and ego. I'm not going to engage in those debates. I'll leave you to read those yourself if you wish.

However, there are several practical guides on how to transcend our ego, start to know ourselves and be authentic. Some of these provide a guide on developing self-awareness. From an academic background, Kent Bach (1974) provides an insight into self-awareness, psychological insecurity, identity and alienation. Nathaniel Branden (2001), a psychotherapist with a PhD in philosophy, approaches self-awareness from the perspective of humanistic and positive psychology. By contrast, Mark Epstein's (1995) view of how to achieve self-awareness draws on his background as a classically trained Freudian psychotherapist who studied Buddhist methods. Therefore, he finds a good deal of common ground with Lama Tsultrim Allione (2008), an international Buddhist teacher. In contrast, Swaraj Wan (2009) presents experiential thoughts on how to know yourself and achieve more in your life.

Deeper self-knowledge is a topic covered by many of the existential authors. They would argue that self-knowledge is an aspiration; a journey that can never be fully completed. Therefore, it is the journey, and the development of ever greater self-knowledge, that is important, not the destination. The existential view of self-knowledge extends beyond self-awareness, our awareness of our patience, emotional responses and characteristics. Self-knowledge focuses on knowing who we are; our values, what we stand for, our deepest beliefs (Nesti, 2004; Valle & Halling, 1989).

Topic-Specific Approaches

The purpose of this book is to help you consistently achieve your peak performance. Peak performances, peak experiences, flow and the zone of optimal functioning are all well-researched areas within psychology and sport psychology. These themes are discussed in Chapter 1. Mihaly Csikszentmihalyi (1990) is the foremost researcher into the phenomena that has been termed *the flow state*. His work examines states of peak performance and peak experience across a wide range of disciplines from a humanistic and positive psychology perspective. Susan Jackson, a sport psychology academic from the University of Queensland, joined forces with Csikszentmihalyi, to apply the principles of *flow* to sports. In addition, researchers such as Yuri Hanin have also researched this area. Hanin developed the concept of the 'zone of optimal functioning', which is reviewed by Dan Gould and Suzie Tuffey (1996). Many of the studies and accounts of peak performances report that performers enter a *mindless* state. Csikszentmihalyi (1990) actually describes flow as a state where we move beyond our self and become unaware of our self. Bob Rotella (2005), an applied sport psychologist who has worked with many of the world's top golfers, also advocates performing in the *mindless state*. In addition, researchers such as Kirstin Flegal and Michael Anderson (2008), from the University of Michigan, have researched the negative effect that overthinking can have on expert performers. Their study examined the effects of overthinking on golf putting performance in 80 golfers and found that performance decreased in experienced players when they were asked to analyze the skill before executing. Malcolm Gladwell (2005) describes how subconscious response is often better than planned or conscious response. This sentiment is echoed by coaches such as Tim Gallwey (1986) and Malcolm Cook (2005). Tim Gallwey advocates that we think less and uses this concept as the basis of his Inner Game coaching methods. The Inner Game approach aims to help performers to 'just do it'. Gallwey identifies that to perform optimally, we need to *trust* ourselves.

All these approaches share common ground. They suggest that we need to perform in a mindless state, so that we can 'just do it'. In order to do that, we need to take our selves beyond any preoccupation with our self and our own thoughts. Being self-conscious, or concerned with self-presentation, interferes with performance (Baumeister, 1993). If we are to let go, and trust our self, we need to be our self. In order to be our self, we need to be happy with our self. To be happy with our self, we need to know our self, which takes us back into our central themes of self-knowledge and authenticity.

The work of Gallwey and Csikszentmihalyi also identifies the importance of focusing on the most important cues in a performance. This is a key principle in Chapter 3. Recently, researchers such as Daniel Weissman (2006), a professor of cognitive perception at the University of Michigan, have identified that we can only focus on one thing at a time. His findings are supported by those of Adam Gazzaley, a neuroscientist from University of California at Berkley (Richtel, 2010). If we are focusing on our own thoughts, or our attention is taken up with our concerns of how we will look or what people will think of us, our focus will not be fully honed in on our performance. There are many who advocate that to hone focus, we tune into our senses. Coaches such as Tim Gallwey (1986) and Malcolm Cook (2005), find common ground with Bob McKim, from Stanford University, who has extensively researched the field of human creativity. McKim states that, "Seeing is encountering reality with all of your being. To encounter reality deeply, you cannot leave part of yourself behind. All of your senses, your emotions, your intellect, your language-making abilities – each contributes to seeing fully" (McKim, 1980).

All of this evidence supports the notion that we perform best when we have a simple, clear focus.

The subjects of focus, concentration and attention have been widely researched in psychology and sport psychology. Texts such as those by Thelma Horn (2008) and that by Jim Taylor and Greg Wilson (2005) provide overviews of the research and theoretical models. Taylor and Wilson (2005) provide an interesting insight into the topic, using perspectives from a researcher, a consultant sport psychologist, a coach and an athlete. Specific research on role clarity in sport is provided by Stuart Bray and Lawrence Brawley (2002), from the University of Waterloo. Csikszentmihalyi (1990) also identifies the importance of clear focus in performance outside of sport. The wider relationship between simplicity, clarity and performance are also covered by writers such as Paul Keller (2009) and Masaaki Imai (1986), who show that they are central to effectiveness in business. Business strategist, Jack Trout, and communications consultant, Steve Rivkin, also highlight the importance of simplicity and clarity in business performance (Trout & Rivkin, 1998).

This evidence illustrates that having a simple, clear focus helps us optimize our performance. Dana Lindsley, from the U.S. Air Force and colleagues from Pennsylvania State University, have identified multi-level links between focus, confidence and increased performance (Lindsley, Brass & Thomas, 1995). Their performance spiral models have been applied to sport by Thelma Horn (2008). These spirals, and the relationships between focus, confidence and motivation are central topics in Chapter 2.

Additional support comes from the work of Albert Bandura (1997), a professor of social science and psychology at Stanford University. He has developed a body of theory which recognizes the importance of *mastery*, in the development of confidence. Bandura's theories of Self-Efficacy underpin many other theoretical models such as Susan Harter's Competence Motivation Theory and Robin Vealey's Sport Specific Model of Self-Confidence. Reviews of these models can be found in sport psychology texts such as Lavallee, Kremer, Moran & Williams (2004). Similar models have been applied to slightly different settings. Gary Dayton (2007), a clinical psychologist with a PhD from Rutgers University, applies a Mindfulness-Acceptance-Commitment (MAC) model to enhancing performance in trading the stock market. The MAC model is an evolution of Cognitive Behavioral Therapy (CBT). Interestingly, the MAC model has been itself researched within sport by Gardner and Moore (2004).

Confidence is widely recognized as a key element in performance and is therefore the focus of Chapter 4. Kate Hayes and her colleagues (2007), recognize that there are many factors that underpin confidence. Much of the sport psychology literature promotes the use of confidence-building techniques, such as goal setting, self-talk, affirmations and imagery. Deborah Feltz's Model of Self-Confidence suggests that confidence can be built on previous performance accomplishments, the vicarious confidence we might gain from others, verbal persuasion, imagined experiences and physiological states (Feltz, Short & Sullivan, 2008). However, those approaches are not included in the recommendations in Chapter 4 (or anywhere else in this book). In my experience the technique-based approaches used in much of sport psychology lead to manufactured confidence, rather than authentic confidence. Techniques such as verbal persuasion highlight that these approaches attempt to convince a person that they are confident. They try to in some way inject the person with confidence from an external source, rather than cultivate it from within. Authors such as Valorie Burton (2007) and Larina Kase (2008) advocate the development of authentic confidence. This comes from knowing who you are (as opposed to focusing on what you do), giving yourself permission to be imperfect, dropping comparison with others and focusing on learning so that you are fully developing your skills (Burton, 2007; Kase, 2008). Applied sport psychologists such as Terry Orlick (2000), also sight factors such as *preparedness* as keys to enhancing confidence and therefore, performance. He has studied the importance of preparedness in multiple disciplines, including sport and medicine.

Theoretical models such as Achievement Motivation, illustrate the links between confidence and motivation. Andrew Elliott, a professor of psychology from the University of Rochester and his peer, Carole Dweck from Stanford University, provide an analysis of achievement motivation and establish the concept of competence as an organizing framework. Motivation is a very well-studied area of psychology and is the focus of Chapter 5. Edward Deci and Richard Ryan, from the University of Rochester, developed Self Determination Theory, a meta-theory comprising five mini theories, which provides a broad framework for the study of human motivation. James Shah, professor of neuroscience at Duke University, and Wendi Gardener, a social psychologist from Northwestern University, provide a critical review of much of this motivational theory (Shah & Gardner, 2008).

Abraham Maslow also developed a theoretical model to explain human motivation. Maslow, a humanistic and developmental psychologist, was one of the first to study psychology from a positive perspective. Rather than researching neurotic behavior and the negative side of mentality, he studied 'exemplary' people such as Albert Einstein. In a sense, he started to take psychology in a new direction. Although his 'hierarchy of needs' model has been criticized, it has been further expanded by many. Maslow's book, *Towards a Psychology of Being* (1998), started to develop his theories in the context of peak performance and peak experiences. Through this development, he also suggests that we need to move beyond ego in order to find peak experiences; a concept that he terms *self-transcendence*.

Specific research has been done on motivation and motives in the workplace by researchers such as James Linder (1998) and Mark Koltko-Rivera (2006). In addition, there is research and theoretical underpinning for the tools that are used in the book. Performance Profiling is grounded in the theory of person-centered therapy, developed by George Kelly in 1955. Its effectiveness has been researched in multiple domains, including sport (Doyle & Parfitt, 2006).

To achieve peak performances consistently, we need to know what contributes to positive performance and also what may detract from or interfere with our performance. Pressure is often sighted as a phenomenon that can negatively affect performance. My take on pressure, which forms the basis of Chapter 6, is significantly different from many researchers, academics and even many applied practitioners in psychology. However, there is support for the notion that if we experience pressure, it is because we have created it in our imagination. Sian Beilock, a professor of psychology at the University of Chicago, suggests that it is our perception of stressful situations that dictates our experience. Many of our existential friends would agree that we choose our lived experiences. Beilock (2010) goes on to explain that even when you construe a situation as threatening, you can perform well. She draws together research from neuroscience and psychology and shows that the body and mind are inextricably linked.

Keith Markman is a professor of psychology at the University of Ohio. He and his colleagues, Julie Suhr and William Klein of Princeton University (2008), integrate theory and research on imagination and the generation of alternative realities. Their work examines mental imagery, thought flow, narrative transportation, fantasizing and counter-factual thinking. When our experience of pressure is related to concerns over future events, that experience is a projection from our imagination. Therefore, these concepts and mechanisms discussed by Markman and his colleagues, provide strong support to the notion that we generate pressure through our imagination.

The reasons why we create this pressure have also been the subject of research. In sport, John Dunn (1999), from the University of Alberta, used a qualitative approach to study the link between perfectionism and competitive anxiety. Tal Ben-Shahar (2009), from the Department of Psychology at Harvard University, sees that this phenomenon extends way beyond sport. He argues that the quest for perfection is not only fruitless but can also lead to unhappiness. Researchers have also drawn links between the uncertainty of outcomes and the perception of pressure. Work on the effect of *uncertainty* on performance can be seen by reading the work of Paul Boelen (2009), from the Department of Clinical Health at the University of Utrecht.

In my work, I have often seen performers struggle when they are relying on their performance to inform their sense of self-worth. If our ego's need to generate positive self-image dominates our reason for performing, we lose sight of the job at hand. Mark Fisher (1998) is a millionaire and author. Using golf as a vehicle, his fictional, semi-autobiographical account provides very practical advice on how to maintain a realistic view of the job at hand. His book helps to show how we often perceive a very simple job as a near impossible feat. Mark Covington (1984), president and chair of psychology at the

University of California at Berkeley, has studied the links between self-worth, fear of failure and reduced performance in education. Existentialists would suggest that if our ego is using our performance to inform our self-worth, it is because we do not have a strong knowledge of our self or sufficient love for our self. Viktor Frankl (1959/1984) writes as a neurologist and psychiatrist, who survived the Holocaust. From his experience in the concentration camp, he argues that we find our reasons to live through finding meaning. Therefore, as humans, we look for meaning in our life experience. If our life is dominated by sport, or business, we develop an identity around that, in order to help us find our meaning. However, Frankl, and many other existential writers, would suggest that genuine fulfillment requires deep self-knowledge and authenticity, rather than living out our labels. These issues are present throughout Chapters 6, 7, 8 and 9.

Our ultimate freedom and choice also dictate how much we test ourselves and push ourselves. It dictates whether we decide to live in our comfort zone or to explore our discomfort zones. Judith Bardwick (1995) recognizes the dangers of residing within the comfort zone. Judith Bardwick is a consultant business psychologist, a fellow of the APA and a former Associate Dean at the University of Michigan. She has written several applied works on the psychology of corporate environments and organizational performance. In addition, Alistair White (2009), a management theorist who writes from a behavioral perspective, provides a framework for understanding the comfort zone and its impact on both performance and development. Other perspectives are provided by Mark Wolfinger and Ralph Heath. Wolfinger (2008) provides an applied perspective from the trading floor of the stock market. Heath (2009) helps illustrates the importance of making mistakes, using his experiences as the founder of an advertising agency, and a committed triathlete. He provides an insight into the way that businesses gain from mistakes (an almost inevitable consequence of operating in our discomfort zone), showing how it underpins confidence and innovation. Further views on creativity and innovation are provided by Robert Weisburg (2006), a cognitive psychologist from Temple University. He examines the creative processes behind Watson and Crick's modeling of DNA and Picasso's painting of *Guernica*, as a basis. Perhaps the most poignant view is offered by existential writer, Rollo May. He cites the importance of courage, when stepping out of the comfort zone, taking risks and being creative (May, 1994).

Many of the concepts that have been discussed, require us to push ourselves and experience stress. Initially, this may seem like an unfortunate consequence, but in reality, it is actually something to be embraced. Hans Seyle (1975) was a pioneering researcher into the phenomena we call stress. He described stress as the body's response to a challenge or demand.

He dismisses the notion that challenging events are unhealthy. Far from it. Seyle notes that 'eustress' (positive stress) is essential for health, describing it as 'the spice of life'. It is perhaps unusual therefore that eustress receives such little attention in psychological literature when compares with distress and anxiety (Le Ferve, Matheny & Kolt, 2003). It could be argued that our experiences of eustress, such as feelings of elation, are fundamental to living a fulfilled life. James Clash (2003), a writer for Forbes magazine, illustrates how this works in practice. His book, *Forbes' To The Limits*, explores the mentality and experience that accompanies feats of extreme human endeavor such as mountaineering, polar exploration, lunar exploration, motor racing and even the development of the H-bomb.

The ability to push oneself and continually raise the bar, is a feature of great performers. Geoff Colvin, Senior Editor at Large for Fortune Magazine, argues that world class performances are the result of focused, deliberate practice. He provides evidence using a variety of research studies, particularly from sport and music. Colvin's arguments are influenced by the work of Anders Ericsson (Ericsson & Charness, 1999) and the models of sport expertise. The underlying proposition is that world class performances are not a product of innate talent, but of hard work and practice. These sentiments are echoed in the autobiographies of successful self-made businessmen and entrepreneurs such as James Caan (2009), Alan Sugar (2010) and Duncan Bannatyne (2006). They are also supported by the biographical account of Warren Buffet's success, provided by Andrew Kilpatrick (2003).

All of this evidence presents us with a consistent message. Neither peak performance, or the strive for self-knowledge and authenticity, can be accomplished at the click of a finger. They take time, application, dedication and often courage. Inevitably it will be uncomfortable. If we aspire to achieve our peak performance consistently, there may be some tough choices that we need to make.

The upside ...?

Your performance and success are ultimately within your control!

Index

A page numbers in *italics* refers to a figure; a number in **bold** refers to a table

Van Gogh, Vincent 26
visualization 13

White, Alistair 78
Wilkinson, Jonny 111–112
winning: and confidence 39; dreams of 26,
27; enjoyment of 15; importance of
23, 53, 61; as motivation 48–50, 55; vs.
not winning 51, 84, 104; vs. performing
well 34; uncertainty of 60

World Championship for
Baristas 11
world class behaviors **105**, 106, 111, 114,
120, 139
World Class Vision: exercise 1 **105**; exercise
2 **105**

zone 8–16, 32; optimal performance
78; pain 72; *see also* comfort zone;
discomfort zone

Printed in the United States
by Baker & Taylor Publisher Services